MW00463958

Understanding **Missouri's**
Constitutional Government

Understanding **Missouri's** Constitutional Government

Richard Fulton and Jerry Brekke

University of Missouri Press   Columbia and London

Copyright © 2010 by
The Curators of the University of Missouri
University of Missouri Press, Columbia, Missouri 65201
Printed and bound in the United States of America
All rights reserved

5 4 3 2 1   14 13 12 11 10

Cataloging-in-Publication data available from the Library of Congress
ISBN 978-0-8262-1903-9

♾™ This paper meets the requirements of the
American National Standard for Permanence of Paper
for Printed Library Materials, Z39.48, 1984.

Designer: Kristie Lee
Typesetter: BOOKCOMP
Printer and Binder: Thomson-Shore, Inc.
Typefaces: Palatino and Novarese

To our wives: Ann and Karen

Contents

Acknowledgments

Special thanks to the folks at the University of Missouri Press, especially Sara Davis and Annette Wenda who helped bring the final version to fruition, and to the reviewers who aided in polishing the final version.

Understanding **Missouri's** Constitutional Government

Introduction

The Federalist Environment

Understanding state and local governments means it is necessary to understand the relationships of these governments to the overall environment of American government. That means having some basic insight into the foundation of that government—its federal nature.

When the founding fathers met in Philadelphia in 1787 to ponder the failures of the prevailing government under the Articles of Confederation, they brought with them baggage full of special interests. Most had as a primary interest the stabilization of the economy and the government, both of which were under great stress following the War of Independence. But that was just the environment of their concerns.

Each of the thirteen states had its own government, of course, that consisted of a legislature, an executive, and a judiciary combined with constitutions that gave local governments autonomy to fulfill basic governmental needs. Since each of the British colonies was administered separately, each developed its own set of rules of the game. When independence came, those rules were redeveloped into new constitutional governments. These documents reflected an evolution based upon British history of the development of limitations on government adopted and adapted by the Americans through the specific mechanism of a single written document: a constitution. And states pioneered and thus mentored this process for the construction of the U.S. Constitution.

A Political Document

Life after the War of Independence was not easy. The colonies, now states, were in financial trouble, as was the Continental government under a weak confederation. Each of the states had its own set of financial regulations, and each had its own monetary system, commercial regulations, and taxes on trade between the states as well as international trade. As a consequence, there was a growing economic depression. With only three major ports (Boston, New York, and Philadelphia) for bringing foreign goods into a country still primarily agricultural, three states had disproportionate influence over the availability of the necessities of domestic life, most of which had to be imported. Transshipment from state to state made the goods too expensive. Commerce was coming to a standstill. Shipbuilders and commercial interests in the Northeast were suffering badly, farmers north and south were having trouble financing their cash crops, and some southern states were having trouble with Indians on their frontiers and needed help from a stronger central government.

Then came Shay's Rebellion, an uprising of farmers against foreclosures on their loans. It necessitated action by the state militia of Massachusetts and seriously alarmed the leadership of all of the states. Remember, they had all just recently risen up against arguably the greatest power on earth and won that struggle, demonstrating the power of an uprising of everyday folks. Add to this that border clashes between states over control of trade on boundary rivers created increased tensions. A need for a uniform set of economic rules possible only with a strengthened central authority became obvious to many leaders throughout the states, especially the leaders of commercial interests. Those who had served in the Continental army and in the Continental Congress also saw survival through a stronger bond between the states.

Thus it was that representatives of the states met in Philadelphia to solve these and other problems—well, all the states but Rhode Island, which evidently was fearful that a stronger central government would disrupt its burgeoning slave trade. The delegates brought with them interests that they were determined to protect; this was to be a political battle, not merely a philosophical one. Broadly speaking, those interests can be categorized into four sets of dual conflicting interests: North versus South, large states versus small states, commercial versus rural and farm interests, and democratic versus republican values.

The constitution that emerged from compromise among these sets of real and persistent interests, then, reflects the concerns of real people within the context of real problems. Remarkably, by sticking to the basic task of creating a structure for a stronger central government and then distributing powers discretely to the national government, the resulting political document worked. Of course, amendments and interpretations have been needed to adapt the Constitution to changing circumstances, but the key foundations have survived to this day. The core of the compromises concluded in 1787 (and 1789 with the addition of the Bill of Rights) remains.

Let us, briefly, indicate the results of some of the key compromises embedded in the new constitution. The large state–small state compromises are perhaps the most visible. The large states wanted to exercise their natural power position by having representation in the legislature based on population. The small states wanted to keep the contemporary arrangement under the Articles of Confederation that gave each state an equal vote. In the end they adopted a bicameral legislature with one house for each interest. And all legislation must pass both houses. Less recognized is that the election of the president also contains this compromise since each state received electoral college votes equal to the number of members of Congress they possessed—two from the Senate plus however many they have in the House of Representatives.

It is still today sad to recall the basic North-South compromises over the institution of slavery. Slavery was sustained in exchange for the end of the importation of slaves. In addition, the South demanded that slaves be counted for membership in the House. The North claimed that the South could not have it both ways; slaves could not be property and also count as citizens. The South, in a strong position since it was needed to form the new union, said, "Why not?" So slaves were counted as three-fifths of a person for purposes of the House membership, and the North got the same count for purposes of taxation. The South was fearful the numerical power of the North would lead it to control the South through threats of export taxes placed on its vital agricultural cash crop. The South also demanded, in return for giving the national government the crucial exclusive powers to regulate interstate and international commerce, that the constitution ban all export taxes levied by Congress.

This last compromise was the key to the demands of the commercial interests. States must give up the right to tax interstate and international commerce. So the commercial-rural interests overlapped with the North-South interests in this instance. Also necessary, of course, was the exclusive issuance of a monetary system by the central government. These as much as anything created a united country.

The conflicts between the democratic and republican forces seem more subtle, but they permeate the final document. Note the small *d* and small *r* in these terms. They are not the present political parties, but the two dominant philosophical viewpoints within the convention. The democratic forces, the so-called Jeffersonians, wanted government close to the citizenry. They championed states' maintaining maximum powers and institutions of government that reflected the more direct voice of the citizens. The forces of republicanism—Hamilton, Washington, and those to be later called the Federalists—wanted a strong central government and more indirect mechanisms of representation.

The development of broad-based democratic elements in American government would come only with time in the form of the expansion of participation for former slaves and for women and nineteen-year-olds (particularly in voting). Other types of restrictions on more direct participation were part of the basic constitutional compromises. Note that the House was to be closer to the citizenry by having lower age qualifications and a short two-year term. They were elected directly by the citizenry. Senators were to be older and serve longer terms. In addition, originally they were chosen by the state legislatures, not directly by the citizens—a republican victory. The republicans had read their Plato and Aristotle and agreed with them that democracy could well descend into mob rule. Even the citizenry needed to be checked and balanced by representative indirectness, including the choosing of the potentially powerful president by an indirect electoral college, not by a direct election.

Of course, the judiciary was formulated completely on republican ideals. The judges were to be appointed by a president indirectly elected by the electoral college and approved by a Senate at first indirectly appointed by state legislatures. Real interests were making a real difference in the form of the new constitution.

Distribution of Powers

The structure of powers within the new centralized government was set by this series of compromises. Three branches were defined with responsibilities checked and balanced so that none would be able to concentrate undue power in its hands. These founding fathers were very concerned about giving too much power not only to the central government but also to any one part of the mechanisms that would govern this new stronger central government.

But the most important part of constructing this new arrangement was to be the division of powers between the central government and the states. Remember, the states had, going into the process, governments with near-sovereign powers in all areas except defense and foreign policy. If they had to form a functioning union that solved the problems accompanying their near-isolationist independence, they would do so by giving

Figure 0.1. **CONSTITUTIONAL DIVISION OF POWERS**

Delegated to the Federal Government

To coin money
To establish post offices and post roads
To grant patents and copyrights
To regulate interstate and foreign
    commerce
To provide for national defense
To conduct foreign policy
To provide for a militia
To govern territories and property
To fix standards of weights and measures

Reserved to the States

To regulate intrastate commerce
To establish local governments
To protect health, safety, and
    morals
To conduct elections
To ratify amendments
To protect life and property and to
    maintain order
All not given to federal or
    prohibited to them

Prohibited by the Federal Government

No tax on exports
Direct taxes must be proportionate
Indirect taxes must be uniform
Cannot violate the Bill of Rights
No preferences to one state
State boundaries cannot be changed
    except with state approval
New states on equal plane
No slavery or titles of nobility

Prohibited by the States

Cannot coin money
No standing army
Cannot enter treaties
No laws impairing obligation
    of contract
Cannot tax imports or exports
Cannot violate federal laws or
    Constitution
No slavery or titles of nobility

Concurrent Powers

Both Congress and states may tax
Both may borrow money
Both may charter banks and corporations
Both may establish courts
Both may make and enforce laws
Both have power of eminent domain
Both may spend for the general welfare

up to the central government only those powers necessary. It is rare in the history of nations for any political unit to give up substantive powers voluntarily. Although the Preamble to the Constitution begins, "We the people . . . ," it is clear that the people were going to operate through the institutions of the states to protect state prerogatives and powers.

The powers of the national government, then, were enumerated (listed specifically), and the powers retained by the states were all those not listed (residual). Of course, some powers had to be prohibited to both, and some powers crucial to governing both needed to be retained (concurrent powers). This is the essence of federalism, the division of powers between two entities within the same nation. Note that local governments are not part of this division of power; they are completely under the responsibility and legal power of the states. What powers they have come from the state constitutions, not from the national constitution.

Figure 0.1 outlines the basic division of powers established by the Constitution between the newly minted federal government and the state governments. Note that although the state lines are equal to the federal lines in number, what is represented is a relatively specific enumeration of powers given to the federal government while the states maintained the broad residue of powers of government particularly as they relate to individuals. Most criminal and civil laws are state laws. States control the overwhelming access to individuals in regards to government programs dealing with health, welfare, public safety, education, roads, and quality-of-life programs—even if, as later proved to be the case, the federal government pays for them. Much of this is performed at the local level, but only at the direction or benevolence of the state constitution. This is why knowledge of state and local governments remains equally if not more important than knowledge of the federal government.

Although the enumerated powers of the federal government listed in Figure 0.1 seem fairly straightforward, there are some that are broader, with less ability to be defined simplistically, or at least have broader implications than the surface would imply. In addition, there are a couple of other phrases in the Constitution that leave an open-ended ability to interpret what powers they convey. The point is that there are some powers in the Constitution that have been the portal for expansion of effective federal power in relation to the states. Because of this use, these powers are often called the "loopholes" in the U.S. Constitution. There are five such basic loopholes:

1. the "necessary and proper" clause
2. the "spending for the general welfare" clause
3. the ability of the federal government to provide for the national defense
4. the "interstate commerce powers" clause
5. the Fourteenth Amendment

The "necessary and proper" clause was activated by the Supreme Court decision in *McCulloch v. Maryland* (1819), which said that the federal government could exercise nonenumerated powers if the new activity (power) was necessary to fulfill the enumerated power. This is called the "implied powers" doctrine and says simply that if the government has the power to do A constitutionally (for example, coin money and tax) and can substantiate that it is necessary to do B (establish a national bank) to fulfill power A, then B is implied in the Constitution by way of the "necessary and proper" clause. Thus, the power to mint money implies the power to establish a bank. This doctrine had been applied to many areas of federal activity by the twenty-first century.

Spending for the general welfare means the federal government can raise and spend money in a variety of areas defined as the general welfare (and what isn't in the general welfare?). So the federal government spends for health, safety, education, and many more areas, even though, remember, the states have the ultimate powers over these areas within their states. So even though the federal government spends billions of dollars on programs through grants-in-aid (Medicaid, welfare programs, roads) and other programs, the states can refuse any spending by the feds within their states and not take the money and the restrictions that come with it. It is a trade-off for the states: money for federal guidance.

National defense provides many areas of federal activities as long as it can be connected to defense—maintaining forts within states, for example, even though the military cannot perform police functions or any other functions within the state without state approval. The Patriot Act is substantiated in part by the ability of the federal government to defend the nation.

The power to regulate interstate commerce and foreign commerce allows the federal government to expand its influence, since advancements in transportation and technology have allowed more and more commerce to be easily carried on across state and national boundaries. What company of any size does not do business across state lines (in interstate or international commerce or both)? Under this power, then, the federal government can, and does, regulate a great many aspects of modern businesses. Note the OSHA provisions that enter the workplace to protect occupational safety and health. The EPA has regulations to protect the environment that touch nearly every commercial entity.

This is not to say that these powers providing expanded activity by the federal government have not been demanded by large segments of the American public. Government has merely responded to demands: when, how, and in what manner is up to the political process of each era. Each person must judge for himself whether, and in what areas, the federal system has provided the national government with too much influence over the life of state and local governments and their citizens.

Last, the Fourteenth Amendment provides the federal government with the responsibility of being the final protector of the rights of Americans under the due process of law and equal protection of the law. Prior to this amendment, the state constitutions provided individuals protections against state government actions, and the national Constitution provided individuals protections against the federal government. The amendment has made the federal government the final protector of individuals under the Bill of Rights, even if (or particularly if) they were violated by state processes. Historical factors minimized the effective use of this amendment until well into the twentieth century. As a result of the broadened use and interpretation of this amendment by the courts and the political system, especially since the mid-twentieth century, the federal government is now actively the final protector of individuals in areas of civil liberties and criminal and civil rights.

Federalism, then, is the fabric of American government. You cannot understand state and local government, or the national government, for that matter, without some basic insight into how federalism works.

1

The Missouri State Constitution

The constitution of Missouri, like all state constitutions, is grounded in the liberal ideals of the Enlightenment writings of Locke, Hume, Rousseau, and others. These ideals were cemented into the American environment in the earliest state constitutions and then into the U.S. Constitution of 1789. The ideals and pragmatic compromises of the founding fathers were not only a result of already extant state constitutions but were also to then echo in the consequent constitutions of the states.

The very concept of a constitution is built on the assumption that power must not only be carefully defined but also be carefully limited by spelling out the responsibilities and limitations of each power-holding center. If government has unlimited powers (as under an authoritarian or divine-right dictator), then constitutions are useless, for constitutions by their very nature define and therefore limit power.

The American Madisonian model limits the powers of government by first dividing the powers between the national government and the states. It further blunts the exercise of power by separating the powers of the three branches of government and then providing checks and balances to ensure no one branch can dominate. And then it insists that even the majority should be limited in its potential to dominate the system. There is no room for tyranny, even of the majority, in the American system. The independent judiciary and the indirect election of the president through the electoral college are prime examples of the reluctance of the U.S. Constitution writers, for example, to create a pure, direct democracy.

As we pursue Missouri's document and its operation, it will not be difficult to see these fundamental doctrines being adopted and adapted.

9

The fundamental Madisonian element adopted in Missouri's constitution has been the concept of the limitation of the power of government. This represents the foundational idea of the social contract: we band together to protect against the whims of unchecked government by producing government by the consent of the governed.

It must be remembered that prior to 1789 the original thirteen states had their own constitutions that were an outgrowth of the charters that outlined government for the colonies under British rule. State experiences expanded the original blueprints, and states continued to experiment with government purpose and organization based on the fact that in forming the Union the states insisted that the federal system leave significant areas of government to the sovereign exercise of the states. It should not come as a surprise then that state constitutions, including that of Missouri, not only reflect elements of the U.S. Constitution but ultimately have formed a history and character all their own.

Protection of individuals from the powers of government was engraved in the early state constitutions and found its way into the U.S. Constitution in its Bill of Rights. The national Bill of Rights, remember, was tacked on to the Constitution only after criticism of its absence. It was needed to complete the state-centered ideal of limiting government's potential for oppression. Although each state's bill of rights already protected individuals from the excess power of the state governments, the national Bill of Rights needed to separately protect individuals from the national government's potential power. Only later, through the Fourteenth Amendment, were the national protections extended to individuals if states were to fall down on this responsibility. Both bills of rights remain operative, of course, but if states do not protect individual rights, the federal government has become the final appeal for protections. At whichever level, the point is clear that limiting government whenever it touches the individual has always been a top priority of American constitutions.

Missouri has lived under four constitutions, the first adopted by a convention on July 19, 1820. It was quite brief and general in its terms, as its function was to be the vehicle for bringing Missouri into the Union as an independent slave state under the terms of the Missouri Compromise, which simultaneously brought Maine's entry as a free state. That constitution was replaced in 1865 by a new document that was known as the "Drake Constitution." This constitution had a strong anti-Confederate orientation. For example, no person who fought for or aided the South during the Civil War was eligible to vote. As a result, this constitution was quite controversial, given the divided loyalties within the state during the

Civil War. The "Ironclad Oath" of fealty to the Union in this constitution that disenfranchised Southern sympathizers was dropped fairly soon, in 1870.

By 1875 the dust of that war began to settle, so there was a referendum held to determine whether the state should hold a convention to formulate a new constitution. The call to a convention won by only 283 votes out of a total 261,670 cast. The consequent convention produced a new constitution that was then submitted to the public for a vote. It was adopted with a more comfortable margin of victory—91,205 to 14,517. Many interests successfully lobbied in the convention, producing a very long and detailed constitution, particularly in the redefining of legislative and executive powers. The document was further burdened by many amendments added over the years. Despite this cumbersomeness, it remained the basic law for the next seventy years.

One of the amendments that was added to the constitution of 1875 required that every twenty years a popular vote should be held on the question of holding a constitutional convention. The bulk and complexity of the 1875 document compounded by its added amendments finally convinced voters that reform was necessary. So at the general election in 1942 the people authorized the calling of a constitutional convention for the purpose of revising the state constitution. Consequently, sixty-eight delegates from thirty-four districts plus an added fifteen at-large delegates, including a mandated equal number from the two political parties (the odd-numbered delegate was an agreed upon non–New Deal Democrat), were chosen to prepare a revision of the constitution of 1875 for voter approval. The majority of the delegates was conservative, with a strong confidence in local self-government and the people, and had a keen interest in maintaining control over public officials.[1]

The convention met on September 21, 1943. Three hundred and seventy-seven proposals were introduced, all suggesting changes to the existing constitution. After months of public hearings, a series of committees examined the proposals and drafted reports. These were considered section by section by the whole convention. Initially, the delegates wanted to rewrite a wholly new constitution; however, the final document contained many of the sections of the constitution of 1875 virtually verbatim. In point of fact, many of the provisions had been parts of the Missouri Constitution of 1820; some fundamentals, it appears, were not subject to the need for much changing. The new constitution was about 11,000 words shorter than the 1875 version; it was determined that some things just did not need to be in the constitution and could be taken care of by statutory law.

The new constitution was submitted to the voters on February 27, 1945. The vote was 312,032 in favor and 185,658 opposed, a strong majority, mitigated by the fact that the turnout at the election was only 20 percent. Therefore, only one-eighth of the eligible voters actually voted in favor of the new constitution. It has endured, nevertheless, to this day.[2]

The constitution retained the right of voters to determine every twenty years whether there should be a call for a constitutional convention. In 1962 voters were given the opportunity to consider a call, as they were in 1982 and 2002, but the propositions were uniformly defeated by over-whelming votes.

Without a major rewrite of the constitution, needed (or wanted) changes had to come through the amendment process. An average of about two amendments a year have been proposed since 1945, voted on usually only at general elections every two years. Around 60 percent of those have been approved, ranging from a complete redo of the judicial article in 1976 and moderate additions like the state lottery to changes of only a few words for a technical adjustment.

The current Missouri Constitution has a length of about 42,100 words. This is above the national average for state constitutions, which run around 30,000 words. In contrast with constitutions of surrounding states, Missouri's is quite large: that of Iowa is 12,500, Kansas's 11,900, Illinois's 13,200, and Nebraska's 20,050. Still other states make Missouri's document look positively brief: Alabama's constitution has 174,000 words, New York's 80,000, and Oklahoma's 68,000.[3] This illustrates the contrasting views of the role state constitutions should play: either a document with multiple specific indicators of state processes and actions or a document of general guidelines to be fleshed out by legislation.

The true importance of the Missouri Constitution, and of other state constitutions, is seldom appreciated because the study of American consti-tutional law has been dominated by a virtually exclusive focus on the U.S. Constitution and its judicial interpretation. Despite this focus, state con-stitutions have historically provided an important influence on not only the development but also the interpretation of the national Constitution. Many of the ideas and structures used in state governments have been included in the national Constitution.[4] For example, bills of rights were often a part of colonial charters. The national Bill of Rights came later as a protection against abuses from that government, abuses already protected under state constitutions. Importantly, the national Constitution under its federalist doctrine leaves broad areas to be regulated by state constitutions and state laws, thus leaving many areas of American life defined by state judiciaries.

There has been in recent years a rediscovery of this role played by state constitutions. State constitutions and state laws have always been decisive in areas of major importance—for example, marital relations and custody cases, property rights and environmental cases, liability cases, taxation and financial cases, cases of all dimensions and variety.[5] A recent development has been the willingness of more and more state courts to construe state constitutional provisions of their bills of rights as guaranteeing to citizens their state's protections in areas or on grounds that may not be allowed under the national Bill of Rights. This has been referred to as new judicial federalism.[6] It is believed by some observers that state courts interpreting state bills of rights may become an important bulwark for individual protection against governmental abuse.[7] The Missouri Constitution serves as a good example of a state constitution that provides extensive possibilities for increased importance, since it is very comprehensive.

The more recent increase in the importance of state constitutions perhaps was best stated by a justice of the Oregon Supreme Court when he noted, "Any defense lawyer who fails to raise an Oregon Constitution violation and relies solely on parallel provisions under the federal constitution . . . should be guilty of legal malpractice."[8] Clearly, a client would be deprived of an opportunity to prevail if the option of a state constitutional claim was not adequately presented or was ignored. The lawyer would, indeed, face possible charges of professional malpractice if a plausible state claim were not raised in the first instance. Most laws, civil and criminal, are state laws, thus the importance of looking to the state constitution and courts first.

Given all this background, a brief look at the contrast between the Missouri Constitution and that of the United States is in order to illustrate the potential it has for expanded citizen protection and interaction with the government. The most obvious difference between the two is their size, as we have already seen. But there are other more important contrasts between state and federal constitutions.

There are some broad contrasts between the national Constitution and Missouri's (and all state constitutions, for that matter) that reflect the foundational concepts of federalism. To begin with, you might notice in comparing state and national constitutions (Figure 1.1) that the focus of the national document is broad, emphasizing fundamental law and structure—a general document. It is succinct and to the point; it sets the structure of

Figure 1.1.

MISSOURI CONSTITUTION VERSUS THE U.S. CONSTITUTION

MISSOURI	UNITED STATES
Very Long	Very Short
Narrow Focus Powers Open	Broad Focus Powers Enumerated
More Philosophical Statements	No Philosophical Statements
Early and Long Bill of Rights	Tacked-on and Short Bill of Rights
Legislative Article Long and Specific Powers	Short and General Powers
Executive Article = Multiple Executive Explicit Bureaucracy	Executive = Singular + VP Bureaucracy to Congress
Judiciary Article Mixed Choice Elected and Appointed	Judiciary Brief and Appointed
Added Article for State Powers Local Government Elections Education Public Employees Taxation	Broad Federal Powers Integrated into Branches
Amendments = Many; Referendums okay	Amendments = Few

government, enumerates the powers of each branch, sets a few elements of federalism while never mentioning the term *federalism* (full faith and credit, privileges and immunities), articulates citizens' rights—and then it quits. There are a few other miscellaneous items and the amendment process, of course, but these are not central to the system and are quickly dealt with. In contrast, the Missouri and other state constitutions have a narrow focus on specifics, many of which it is often argued would better be left to ordinary statutory law—they are documents of multiple specific indicators. Much of this is necessary to facilitate the numerous important areas of responsibility left to the states in our federal system. The next-to-bottom element of contrasts in Figure 1.1 illustrates this point by indicating a few of the articles in the constitution of Missouri that deal with particular powers, powers that states must institutionalize, as they are their areas of supremacy (local government, elections, education) or are shared but discreet responsibilities (taxation, spending). In contrast, the U.S. Constitution simply and succinctly integrates its enumerated powers within its first two articles (legislative and executive).

The legal theory of government is also different between the two constitutions. The national Constitution, in theory—and putting aside the "loopholes" and interpretation and use discussed in the introduction that mitigate the fact—assumes the national government has only those powers invested in it by the Constitution. In stark contrast, state governments assume that their powers, reflected in their constitutions, extend to all areas not specifically prohibited to them. Note the Tenth Amendment to the U.S. Constitution, which specifically reserves powers not mentioned in the document to the states. Even given this, however, most states, unlike the national government, use their broad power of discretion in such a way as to limit their own range of activities, thus not taking advantage of all the possibilities open to them. For example, most state financial articles set limits on their state government's actions in the area of powers to tax and to incur debt, and much state power is allocated to local governments, giving them a degree of local autonomy. All states prohibit debt financing of their operational budgets. The Missouri Constitution, as we shall see, is a good example of this general trait of state constitutions, that of requiring very specific limits on its own scope and uses of governmental authority. These are dramatically different legal assumptions upon which the two levels of government operate. Courts and politics continually spar over the limitation of the powers of the federal government. On the other hand, states may be able to do what they please in many areas, but they usually please to limit their governments.

There is a caveat to these theories, however, and that is reflected in the *supremacy clause* of the U.S. Constitution. This states that the national Constitution is the supreme law of the land, leaving state constitutions subordinate to that Constitution and to federal law. We must be clear, however, that this clause applies only to those powers enumerated in the national Constitution and as expanded, to be sure, by the courts. But this clause most definitely does not apply to the rest of the powers of government given to, not prohibited to, or left to the states. We forget that states must give permission for the federal government to do much of what it does within the boundaries of the states, from welfare spending to disaster support, even if the federal government is paying for these services. It is quite important to remember that in these areas the states are supreme. It only appears as if the federal government has these powers because

Figure 1.2.		
CONTRASTING STATE CONSTITUTIONAL ARTICLES		
WITH MISSOURI ARTICLES		
CONSTITUTION OF MISSOURI		**ARTICLES IN OTHER STATES**
		NOT FOUND IN MISSOURI'S
Article I	Bill of Rights	Militia
Article II	The Distribution of Power	Recall
Article III	Legislative Department	Collective Bargaining
Article IV	Executive Department	Boundaries
Article V	Judicial Department	Conservation
Article VI	Local Government	Reapportionment
Article VII	Public Officers	Agriculture
Article VIII	Suffrage and Elections	Livestock
Article IX	Education	Usury
Article X	Taxation	Labor Relations
Article XI	Corporations	Public Housing
Article XII	Amending the Constitution	Public Utilities
Article XIII	Public Employees	Motor Vehicles
		Immigration and Labor
		Public Indebtedness
		Public Finance
		Encouragement of Literature, Trade
		Oaths, Bribery of Elections
		Environment

states seldom refrain from taking federal moneys in exchange for following whatever strings are attached to the money.

There is one last general point to be made about the various powers states possess and how they incorporate those powers into their constitutions. Missouri's choices in how to organize the distribution of its particularized powers within the constitution will be discussed in detail within subsequent chapters, but remember that states organize their constitutions differently. They put things where other states do not; they make certain aspects of state life separate articles, while other states incorporate those same aspects within the specifics of other titled articles. For our purposes now it might simply be instructive to give an indication of how states organize their constitutions quite differently.

All, of course, include quite early in their documents a bill of rights followed by philosophical statements and articles covering the three branches of government (though each state still has its idiosyncrasies even within these basic sections). In Figure 1.2 we can see the organization of the articles of the Missouri Constitution contrasted with some of the articles that are used to organize other state constitutions but are not found in Missouri's—at least as separate articles. The simple point in this illustration is that many states utilize separate articles for topics some of which may well be embodied within the Missouri Constitution but not as separate articles. Thus, Missouri's Bill of Rights talks about collective bargaining within one of its sections, but a couple of states use a separate article to provide this discussion.

Without going into each state's differences, Figure 1.2 gives some idea of the diversity of topics thought important to highlight by different states within their constitutions. Several topics of those listed are not covered at all in the Missouri document but are left to statutory law. The encouragement of literature and trade, for example, is in the Massachusetts Constitution but in no other, certainly not Missouri's.

Some topics reflect the history or economy of the state that uses them. Agricultural articles are prominent in largely agricultural and rural states, as are mining articles in states with a historic dependence on mining industries. A couple of western states find water resources a significant topic for the development and growth of their states, and thus they establish rules on this topic as a separate article. Here, as in all political documents, we can see the interests prominent within states at least at the time of the writing or rewriting of the state constitutions. In some cases, the amendment process has added new concepts or interests to the state documents, even as separate articles, as we see in the case of state lotteries in some state constitutions. Again, many of the separate articles in other state constitutions are readily found in Missouri's but not highlighted as separate articles. The militia, public indebtedness, labor, and reapportionment are all obvious examples. The simple point remains that state constitutions have much in common, but from size to content they also reflect the unique character of each state.

2

The Bill of Rights
and Distribution of Powers

When we refer to the philosophical elements of the constitution in Figure 1.1, what we mean is that there are statements of principle and ideals placed in the Missouri Constitution that are virtually absent from the U.S. version. The first of these statements reflects the fact that Missouri, as are most states, is explicit about its appeal to a higher power as the foundation of the state. For example, the Preamble to the Missouri Constitution states that the people establish the constitution "with profound reverence for the Supreme Ruler of the Universe, and grateful for His goodness." Such overt reference to a higher power is nowhere evident in the national Constitution. Although it is true that the preamble is not technically a part of the legal document, the Missouri Constitution as we shall see incorporates other references to the Almighty within its Bill of Rights that do raise the aura of the appeal to a creator as the formation of government.

The writers of the U.S. Constitution were mindful of the necessity of passing the document through thirteen disparate states and thus did not want to put anything in the document that might endanger its passage. Its curt language was to omit anything not directly to the point of settled compromises. Not even agnostics were to be offended if it could be avoided, and so they took seriously separation of religion and state. Nor was a civic philosophy put in the federal Constitution; the fundamentals of liberal philosophy (for example, government by consent of the governed) were assumed, and the founding fathers did not want to dicker over language to explain them in the Constitution so they simply omitted any philosophical content.

Yet the early articles of the Missouri Bill of Rights are, as we shall see, explicit in the civic beliefs of the people of the state. Nothing was to be left to the imagination of less dedicated democrats, so the ideals of American (Missouri) government are laid out for all to see. You will notice particularly in the first four sections of the constitution that the writers wanted to incorporate the fundamental elements of the liberal philosophy of government in overt terms. "Government originates with the people and is for their good only" is the first premise of the state's view of government (Section 1 of the Bill of Rights).

Section 2 spells out these principles by ensuring that people have "a natural right to life, liberty, the pursuit of happiness and enjoyment of the gains of their own industry." The federal Constitution in practice if not in these specific words protects life, liberty, and property and leaves the propaganda phrase that includes happiness to the Declaration of Independence. Still, this section emphasizes equality under the law for all and protection of industry, and that most definitely was to include property rights. This section and the third ensure the citizens that government belongs to them and they can change it if it does not fulfill its responsibilities.

States jealously guard their sovereign rights, so it is that Section 4 of the Missouri Bill of Rights specifies that Missouri is "a free and independent state" subject only to the U.S. Constitution. And if it is ever proposed to change that Constitution in a way that affects the rights or powers of citizens or local governments, then the people have a right to approve those amendments and to do so directly.

The first concern of the Missouri Constitution, then, is to state the concepts sustaining a free people within a limited government, none of which the writers of the U.S. Constitution felt a necessity to include.

When we discuss the Bill of Rights in detail below we shall see how states expand upon the protections available to their citizens, not only by explaining the rights and their limitations in more detail but also by including many areas as "rights" not included in the federal version. Missouri is much more specific in articulating the rights of individuals. In many cases in giving these rights the Missouri Constitution expands upon the area of rights by specifying the limits to those rights. Generally, the limits reflect what the U.S. Supreme Court has done to define the broad statements of rights in the national Constitution. This is true particularly concerning the U.S. First Amendment. Mostly what is explained is that you can exercise the rights of free speech, press, religion, and assembly, as long as you do not interrupt or harm the rights of others in these areas.

Note, for example, that while the national First Amendment simply states that Congress shall make no law concerning the areas of speech, press, religion, and assembly, the Missouri Bill of Rights uses three sections alone to talk about religion and has separate sections for other rights.

In each chapter of this book we will take a close look at each article of the Missouri Constitution for the purposes of specific analysis. Here we look at the legal foundations of the Bill of Rights of the Missouri Constitution and discuss each of the sections of that article. What we want to accomplish in this part of the chapter is a discussion of the meaning of these sections and in some cases to contrast them with and show their relationship to the national Constitution. Many sections of the Bill of Rights illustrate how state constitutions can provide extra areas of protection not in the U.S. Bill of Rights. Thus, states have often proved more creative by articulating specific rights that citizens have felt needed increased protection by being raised out of the level of statutory law and into the more fundamental arena of the Bill of Rights.

The perception has been that when the issues contained in a bill of rights are considered, attention must be focused on the national Constitution and its first ten amendments. Yet state constitutions contain bills of rights that protect specific rights and do so in the first instance. Since most police, criminal justice, and judicial systems are under the responsibility of the state and most law is state law, then the first line of defense for rights protections must be from the state constitutional judicial system.

Conrad Paulsen observed in a 1951 issue of the *Vanderbilt Law Review,* "Although state constitutions contain a full statement of our civil liberties, on the whole the record of state guardianship of First Amendment Freedom is disappointing. . . . If our liberties are not protected in Des Moines the only hope is in Washington." However, by at least the 1970s there had been a rediscovery of state constitutional protections, and state courts began deciding cases based on state rather than federal constitutional provisions. In 1986 United States Supreme Court Justice William J. Brennan recognized this trend by noting that "rediscovery of state supreme courts of the broader protections afforded their own citizens by their state constitutions . . . is probably the most important development in constitutional jurisprudence of our time."[1]

This trend has continued to grow, despite the traditional reliance on—and media exposure of—the application of the national Constitution. The supremacy clause of the Constitution does not mean that the national law is supreme in all fields, it is worth repeating; it is only supreme when the national government has authority under the Constitution. State constitutional law is supreme when it is not in conflict with the national Constitution, constitutional national laws, or treaties. This is particularly apt when state declarations of rights do not duplicate the national Bill of Rights. Thus, state declarations of rights have their own authority, which makes them subject to independent state interpretation. Indeed, state constitutions can be more protective of rights than can their national counterpart, and they can, and do, include rights that are excluded from the national Constitution.

To the extent that the Missouri Constitution might confer constitutional protection to rights not recognized at the national level, another forum for the redress of grievances is added to the citizenry. In addition, if the national interpretation of certain rights were to change, Missouri courts could still maintain their stronger protections of those rights under the state constitution. Let's take a close look at Article I, following which we will discuss the one-paragraph Article II.

Article I:
The Bill of Rights in the Constitution

Article I of the Missouri Constitution is the Bill of Rights. It could well be argued that by its very placement the writers emphasized that the first task of government is the protection of individual rights—and thus limitation of government powers. It is our present task to state and then briefly analyze the thirty-four sections of this article with special emphasis upon the legal foundations of the protections as reflected not only in the words but in their interpretation by the courts as well. Only in this chapter do we quote the Missouri Constitution section by section followed by analysis. It is because of the centrality of these rights to citizenship that we give this part of the constitution such close scrutiny.

Section 1: Source of Political Power—Origin, Basis, and Aim of Government

That all political power is vested in and derived from the people; that all government of right originates from the people, is founded upon their will only, and is instituted solely for the good of the whole.

This is in large part a restatement of the preamble, which states that the constitution is established to provide for the better government of the state on the basis of the theoretical foundations of our system. This means primarily the proposition of social contract theorists Locke and Rousseau that government is established exclusively by the consent of the people. There has not been much court elaboration of this section, although in a 1967 case the Supreme Court of Missouri noted that legislative power comes from the people (as the closest to the people): "The General Assembly, unless restrained by the constitution, is vested in its representative capacity with all of the primary power of the people."[2]

Section 2: Promotion of General Welfare—Natural Rights of Persons— Equality under the Law—Purpose of Government

That all constitutional government is intended to promote the general welfare of the people; that all persons have a natural right to life, liberty, the pursuit of happiness and the enjoyment of the gains of their own industry; that all persons are created equal and are entitled to equal rights and opportunity under the law; that to give security to these things is the principal office of government, and that when government does not confer this security, it fails in its chief design.

The Missouri Constitution reflects a great deal of the ideology of American government, as illustrated by this section. This section provides two basic responsibilities of government. The first is a general philosophical objective that recognizes the concept that one purpose of government is the general welfare of the people, and a government that does not safeguard that welfare does not meet its major obligation. This might bring to mind Lincoln's assertion that government should be "of the people, by the people, and for the people."

The U.S. Declaration of Independence is the origin of the life, liberty, and happiness phrase here, although the substance of the U.S. Constitution emphasizes protection of life, liberty, and property. Not to let this point drop, this section adds the protection "of the gains of their own industry"—of property. Protecting these "natural rights" is the second fundamental function of government and is combined with the protection of equal rights and opportunities under law. In the national Constitution the Fourteenth Amendment's due process and equal protection clauses offer the same broad protections. In fact, federal courts have often used these clauses to protect individuals against state government action not checked by the state courts. These clauses in the Missouri Constitution have not had the impact on state court activity that the national clauses through the national courts have had.

In 1964, however, the Supreme Court of Missouri considered a challenge to a Sunday closing law. The charge was that it was unconstitutional by being a special law, containing unreasonable, arbitrary, and discriminating classification in that "persons are created equal; and are entitled to equal rights and opportunities under the law."[3] The court ruled that the forced closings did not violate the due process and equal protection clauses of the Missouri Constitution.

Another Missouri case dealt with the enjoyment of the gains of one's own industry. The Supreme Court interpreted this provision as not prohibiting the inclusion of compulsory union membership provisions in collective bargaining agreements.[4]

Generally speaking, the Missouri Supreme Court interprets the equal rights and opportunities clauses here as having the same meaning as the equal protection clause of the Fourteenth Amendment of the national Constitution. Both are intended to prevent invidious discrimination. In pursuing this goal, the crucial consideration is whether the classification burdens a "suspect class" or impinges on a "fundamental right." "Fundamental rights" include, but are not limited to, freedom of speech, freedom of press, freedom of religion, the right to vote, and the right to personal privacy, all of which are enumerated later in the Bill of Rights. Still, in one case the state was interpreted to be able to restrict political conduct by prohibiting state merit employees from being candidates for any partisan office, determining that exclusion based on this law served a valid and rational state interest.[5]

A "suspect class" would be one defined by race, national origin, or in some cases illegitimacy that because of historical unequal treatment evokes special protection from a political process controlled by the majority.[6] A case in 1993 challenged a parole denial on the basis of equal protection. The plaintiffs submitted a list of inmates, the crimes committed, and the amount of time served before parole had been granted. The argument was that inmates with similar crimes should be given parole within the same time period. The list did not include details of the crimes, so the court could not make a comparison as to the seriousness of the crimes. The court stated that the plaintiffs had not shown that they and the inmates included on the list were similarly situated, and noted that prisoners and parole classifications did not involve suspect classes or fundamental rights. Therefore, the classification made in granting parole had to be only rationally related to a legitimate government purpose. Note the use of government purpose as a rationale to justify government action. Requiring prisoners who commit

more serious crimes to serve more time in prison was a legitimate government purpose. The court ruled that the plaintiffs had not shown any equal
protection violation—or prejudicial treatment.[7]

It is not clear whether the equal rights and due process clauses contained in Section 2 apply only to governments or whether there may be
some application to private actors. How could it protect against private
actions? "If these provisions are construed to impose an affirmative governmental duty to prevent discriminatory action by non-governmental
actors, they could have the same effect as an equality guarantee directly
enforceable against private infringers."[8]

Section 3: Powers of the People over Internal Affairs, Constitution, and Form of Government

*That the people of this state have the inherent, sole and exclusive right to regulate
the internal government and police thereof, and to alter and abolish their constitution and form of government whenever they may deem it necessary to their safety
and happiness, provided such change be not repugnant to the Constitution of the
United States.*

Again, this is a basic statement of the power of the people, which would
be absolute except for the national Constitution. There is a restriction on
the form of government that might be established since a republican or
representative form of government is required by Article IV, Section 4, of
the national Constitution. The section would appear to allow for initiatives
to alter the constitution as is later explicitly placed in the constitution.

Section 4: Independence of Missouri—Submission of Certain Amendments to the Constitution of the United States

*That Missouri is a free and independent state, subject only to the Constitution of
the United States; that all proposed amendments to the Constitution of the United
States qualifying or affecting the individual liberties of the people or which in any
wise may impair the right of local self-government belonging to the people or which
in any wise may impair the right of local self-government belonging to the people of
this state, should be submitted to conventions of the people.*

Section 4 recognizes the supremacy of the national Constitution while
affirming the rights of the state as a sovereign body. States are fond of

reminding citizens that they are the foundational government with rights of the national government being only those specified in the Constitution. However, the statement that requires amendments dealing with individual liberties or the right of self-government to be submitted to conventions of the people is trumped by the national Constitution. It states that ratification by state legislatures is valid, as well as by conventions. Yet it is still important to note that individual liberties and local self-government were deemed so important that constitutional changes in these areas needed direct input by citizens through a convention.

We see that Sections 1–4 of Article I are basically confined to general statements of principles; they provide broad guidance in the area of the relationship of people to the government. Principles can be important, however, as noted in a court case in 1942 in which the Supreme Court of Missouri considered the concept of privacy and related the right of privacy to the principles stated in these sections. The basis for the right to privacy or personality was viewed as the right to be left alone, a part of the right to liberty and pursuit of happiness, which recognizes that the individual does not exist solely for the state or society but has inalienable rights that cannot be lawfully taken from him so long as he behaves properly.[9]

In 1988 the state supreme court heard the case of Nancy Cruzan, who had been severely injured in a car accident and left in a vegetative state. The court reversed a trial court and considered what rights an individual has in these conditions by stating that the state has no right "to force an individual to die by starvation and dehydration," though there was a right to refuse treatment. Strict procedures were needed to prove that consent, however, and these were not met in the Cruzan case. At the same time the court declined to find a broad right to privacy in applying the common law right to informed consent. The U.S. Supreme Court, on appeal, affirmed that a competent person has the right to informed consent under due process of law, but it does not apply to incompetent persons.[10] The right to privacy remains a slippery concept.

Section 5: Religious Freedom—Liberty of Conscience and Belief—Limitations

That all men have a natural and indefeasible right to worship Almighty God according to the dictates of their own consciences; that no human authority can control or interfere with the rights of conscience; that no person shall, on account of his religious persuasion or belief, be rendered ineligible to any public office or trust or profit in this

state, be disqualified from testifying or serving as a juror, or be molested in his per-
son or estate; but this section shall not be construed to excuse acts of licentiousness,
nor to justify practices inconsistent with the good order, peace or safety of the state,
or with the rights of others.

As we embark upon the discussion of particularized rights in the Missouri Bill of Rights, it is important to realize that the state constitution is much more specific and deals separately with elements of protections given more efficiently in the U.S. Constitution. At the very beginning here we see that the Missouri Constitution gives separate sections to the two religion-related rights that are given but two phrases in the First Amendment of the national version. This conflicting pattern will recur with subsequent rights. State constitutions spell out the rights (and often the limits upon those rights) that are generalized and need more court interpretation in the case of the national Constitution.

Section 5, then, clearly mandates freedom of worship—within the context of conscience—not being a factor in relations with government. Religious belief cannot disqualify anyone from public office or from serving on juries, nor can it affect their property rights. Unlike the national Constitution, though, this section notes limits upon these rights. A balance must be found that protects individual religious freedom while at the same time allowing the rights of the larger community to be considered. Believe what you will, but when you begin to practice your beliefs, there are limits that protect others' rights and the solemnity of the community.

A case from 1973 offers an example of a challenge based on a reading of this section. In it an argument was made that the payment of real and personal property taxes that support public schools by parents who sent their children to a religiously oriented school interfered with their constitutional right to select such a school for their children. The argument was that paying taxes and private school tuition placed an unfair burden on the family. The Supreme Court of Missouri found that the paying of taxes did not interfere with religious freedom even if it might cause some financial burden.[11]

Another case dealt with members of a religious society who sought to nullify a zoning regulation that denied them access to housing on the basis that they did not qualify for an area zoned for single-family residences. The Supreme Court of Missouri found that denial of a permit to make their home in a residence existing in an area zoned single-family residential was not a violation of their constitutional rights under the freedom to worship clause. The needs of the religious organization did not take precedence over the rights of the community to maintain areas for single-family residences.[12]

Section 6: Practice and Support of Religion Not Compulsory— Contracts Therefore Enforceable

That no person can be compelled to erect, support or attend any place or system of worship, or to maintain or support any priest, minister, preacher or teacher of any sect, church, creed or denomination of religion; but if any person shall voluntarily make a contract for any such object, he shall be held to the performance of the same.

This section is also directed toward the separation of church and state and has been interpreted by the Missouri courts to demand a stronger barrier than does the national Constitution. The state supreme court held in 1974 that a state law requiring public school boards to provide textbooks to teachers in private schools violated Section 6 since this section prohibits the support of any "teacher or sect." In addition, the provision requiring that textbooks be provided to pupils attending private schools was found in violation of Article IX, Section 8, of the Missouri Constitution, which prohibits payment from a public fund in aid of any religious creed, church, or sectarian purpose. This is clearly a more restrictive view of the permissible use of public funds than is allowed under current precedent by the U.S. Supreme Court if there is no excessive government entanglement with religion.[13]

The Missouri Constitution is also more restrictive in terms of the use of public funds for transportation of children to private schools. The Supreme Court of Missouri ruled as early as 1953 that the use of public funds to transport pupils to and from sectarian parochial schools was not permissible since it was not for the purpose of maintaining free public schools (a constitutional responsibility), and a school's funds must be used solely for maintaining free public schools. This was after, it should be noted, the federal Supreme Court had allowed this practice under the rationale that providing safe transportation was aiding a child and not a religion. The Missouri court's position was accepted by the U.S. Supreme Court in a memorandum opinion in 1974, in which the Court affirmed the denial of transportation on public school buses to parochial children, noting that the state had a valid interest in maintaining a very high wall separating church and state.[14] Section 7 will reaffirm this concept.

Section 7: Public Aid for Religious Purposes—
Preferences and Discriminations on Religious Grounds

That no money shall ever be taken from the public treasury, directly or indirectly, in aid of any church, sect or denomination of religion, or in aid of any priest, preacher, minister or teacher thereof, as such; and that no preference shall be given to nor any discrimination made against any church, sect or creed of religion, or any form of religious faith or worship.

In a sense, Section 7 sums up Sections 5 and 6, emphasizing again the separation of church and state and free exercise of religion. An example of an application of this section was seen in a case in which the Supreme Court of Missouri ruled that no judicial officer may base a determination of child custody on approval or disapproval of the belief, doctrine, or tenets of the religion of either parent.[15]

Thus, the concept of religious freedom in the state of Missouri is a result of the application of both the Missouri and the national constitutions. One way to involve the federal government has been through the use of funds to preempt state powers. For example, if federal funds are involved, the U.S. Supreme Court has held that—provisions of the state constitution notwithstanding—educationally deprived children attending nonpublic schools are entitled to receive an allocation of federal funds for programs of special service comparable in quality, scope, and opportunity to those received by children in public schools.[16]

Section 8: Freedom of Speech—Evidence of Truth in
Defamation Actions—Province of Jury

That no law shall be passed impairing the freedom of speech, no matter by what means communicated: that every person shall be free to say, write or publish, or otherwise communicate whatever he will on any subject, being responsible for all abuses of that liberty; and that in all suits and prosecutions for libel or slander the truth thereof may be given in evidence; and in suits and prosecutions for libel the jury, under the direction of the court, shall determine the law and the facts.

This section has not provoked much in the way of interpretation from the Supreme Court of Missouri. Protections and restrictions concerning freedom of speech and slander and libel are basically the result of case law interpreting the national Constitution. Any reference to the Missouri Constitution is usually in conjunction with an interpretation of the national Constitution. For example, in a 1960 case the Supreme Court of Missouri upheld a statute providing for the seizure of obscene materials, stating that there was not a violation of the free speech and press, privileges and immunities, or due process provisions of either the Missouri Constitution or the national Constitution. Illustrating the supremacy of the national Constitution in the area of individual rights, the case was appealed to the U.S. Supreme Court, where the Missouri ruling over this case's specifics was reversed.[17]

In 1989 the Missouri court upheld a law that prohibited the promotion of obscenity. The court noted that previous decisions as early as 1896 had ruled that obscene publications were outside the scope of constitutionally protected speech. The 1896 decision was based on Section 14 of the 1875 constitution, and this provision was virtually adopted whole by the 1945 revision—this section of the current constitution. The antiobscenity statute was upheld using the standards provided by the national Supreme Court in *Miller v. California*. The basic federal guidelines remain: (1) whether the average person, applying contemporary standards, would find the work, taken as a whole, appeals to prurient interests; (2) whether the work depicts or describes in a patently offensive way sexual conduct specifically defined by the applicable state law; and (3) whether the work, taken as a whole, lacks serious literary, artistic, political, or scientific value.[18]

In another 1989 case the Supreme Court of Missouri answered an argument that speech protection under the state constitution was broader than under the national Constitution and protected solicitation by prostitutes. In response the court stated, "Where the state has exercised its inherent police power and criminalized prostitution, the constitutional guarantee of freedom of speech is not violated when the speech claiming protection has as its objective an unlawful, economically motivated act." In a 1992 case the Missouri court ruled that a state statute regulating the use of outdoor advertising on private property adjacent to the interstate and primary highway systems did not impair business's right to freedom of expression. Such regulation was a valid exercise of the state's police power, and the regulation was necessary to promote highway safety, convenience, and enjoyment of highway travel and to preserve the natural scenic beauty of highways and adjacent areas. This was a valid exercise of police power to protect public safety, health, and morals. The law was also ruled content neutral; it was not affected by what the advertisement said.[19]

The court balanced the interests of government and individuals in violation of free speech in a case involving the rules of professional conduct concerning the disciplining of an attorney. A prosecuting attorney was charged with making "a statement with reckless regard as to its truth or falsity" concerning the presiding judge in a murder case. The court ruled that the attorney could not use freedom of speech as a defense against violations of the Rules of Professional Conduct. The state's interest in maintaining public confidence in the administration of justice was a compelling governmental objective that justified the restriction on freedom of speech.[20]

Another distinction was made in terms of speech versus conduct in a case involving a state law that outlawed the practice of using prizes and other considerations by real estate brokers to promote the purchase of real property. The court upheld the law as a regulation of conduct, not of speech.[21]

Section 9: Rights of Peaceable Assembly and Petition

That the people have the right peaceably to assemble for their common good, and to apply to those invested with the powers of government for redress of grievances by petition or remonstrance.

The basic meaning of this section depends on the interpretation of the assembly provisions of the First Amendment of the national Constitution. For example, when an individual urged a crowd at a protest rally to do violence against officers of the law and certain others during a period of racist tension, he was prosecuted under Missouri statutes. The prosecution was challenged as a violation of the right of assembly under the U.S. First Amendment. The appeal was denied under the logic that prosecution under Missouri law was warranted because the state has a strong and legitimate interest in preventing mob violence.[22] Note that the Missouri Constitution, like many other state constitutions, does not specify the application of assembly rights just to government interference—as does the national Constitution. Thus, an interpretation of this clause could be conceived that would provide a greater protection from potential infringement of the rights of peaceable assembly and petition than available from the federal Constitution.

Section 10: Due Process of Law

That no person shall be deprived of life, liberty or property without due process of law.

Readers should recognize this fundamental protection from the Fifth and Fourteenth Amendments of the national Constitution that have given rise to some of the most important court decisions restricting the powers of government. What "due process" generally means, both at the national and at the state levels, is that governmental action that denies a person life, liberty, or property must be done in a fundamentally fair and consistent manner. What is or is not "fair," of course, is up to court interpretation, which has given the courts great power in controlling the other branches of government in their relationships with individuals. Criminal cases are fertile ground for the application of due process, and they are constantly being examined by the courts. In an early example from 1953, the Missouri court found that the circumstances under which a defendant of low intelligence had confessed guilt (a confession coerced by inspired fear or promise of protection and daily interrogation over long periods of detention) were fundamentally unfair—and thus declared unconstitutional under the due process clause of the federal Fourteenth Amendment.[23]

Note that it is the federal Fourteenth Amendment that provides the basic thrust of both state and national court interpretations of due process. In 1990 the Missouri Supreme Court was faced with a due process argument concerning the Commission of Retirement, Removal, and Discipline of Judges. Even though the commission commingles the functions of investigation, prosecution, and adjudication, the court ruled that a judge was not denied due process by a decision of the commission. It said the commission would recommend discipline only after a formal hearing in which the key elements of due process were observed: assistance of counsel, notice, cross-examination of witnesses, and the introduction of evidence.[24]

The following fourteen articles articulate the specific areas of due process of law protected by the Missouri Constitution. They generally echo, and are anchored within, the criminal due process areas protected within the national Constitution. Much of the court precedent in defining the reach of each protection comes from federal cases, so we will focus on the reflections of these and the expansions allowed within the Missouri Constitution.

Section 11: Imprisonment for Debt

That no person shall be imprisoned for debt, except for nonpayment of fines and penalties imposed by law.

This provision goes back to the colonial experience and has been a traditional restriction on government; however, as with most constitutional law, there are always questions as to the application. The Missouri court ruled that imprisonment for contempt of court was a proper remedy for failure to comply with a court order for the maintenance of child support, when a person disobeyed the order by intentionally placing himself in a position that made compliance impossible.[25] This section is a case where a state constitution is more specific in the terms of the right than is the national Constitution.

Section 12: Habeas Corpus

That the privilege of the writ of habeas corpus shall never be suspended.

Though protected by the national Constitution, of course, the role of habeas corpus in the Missouri justice system is summed up by the following: "The privilege of the writ of habeas corpus shall never be suspended, and neither this court nor any other court has the right to interfere with the exercise of that right by individuals."[26] A writ is a court order directing an official who has a person in custody to bring the individual before a judicial official and justify the detention. In Missouri, twenty-four hours is the normal time a person can be held in jail without a stated cause.

Section 13: Ex Post Facto Laws—Impairment of Contracts—Irrevocable Privileges

That no ex post facto law, nor law impairing the obligation of contracts, or retrospective in its operation, or making any irrevocable grant of special privileges or immunities, can be enacted.

The basic thrust of these restraints is to limit state authority in the use of legislation in regard to individuals. The ex post facto clause is aimed at laws that are retroactive and either alter the definition of crimes or increase the punishment for criminal acts already committed.[27] The other provisions basically force governments to pass general laws that fit categories of individuals, and thus prevent government from using laws either to interfere with private contracts or to favor specific individuals or corporations.[28] Retrospective laws are defined as laws that "take away or impair a right acquired under existing laws." An example of this was a childhood sexual abuse statute that authorized causes of action that had been barred due to the existing statute of limitations. The Missouri Supreme Court ruled that once the original statute of limitations expires, thus barring action, a defendant acquired a vested right to be free from suit and that any retrospective legislative revival of the case would be unconstitutional.[29] But after the particularly horrendous sexual abuse death of a child (Megan), the legislature passed a law requiring individuals who had been previously convicted of or pled guilty to sex crimes (subject to the law's requirements) to register as sex offenders. The Missouri Supreme Court said that this law did not violate the ex post facto or due process of law clauses of the state constitution.[30]

Section 14: Open Courts—Certain Remedies—Justice without Sale, Denial, or Delay

That the courts of justice shall be open to every person, and certain remedy afforded for every injury to person, property or character, and that right and justice shall be administered without sale, denial or delay.

This is a rather clear-cut statement of principle in terms of the role that the courts are to play in the operation of justice in the state of Missouri. An illustration of the application of this clause occurred when the Supreme Court of Missouri held a law unconstitutional that required any person having a malpractice claim against a health care provider to refer the claim to the secretary of the Professional Liability Review Board Authority before filing an action in court. This was held to be a precondition to access to the courts and, thus, a violation of this provision.[31] However, the court did not find a violation of this section when a medical malpractice plaintiff had to file, within ninety days of filing a complaint, an affidavit stating the health provider's opinion of the merit of the complaint. This procedure was justified by the court as an aid to the court in freeing itself from frivolous malpractice suits.[32]

In another case, the court allowed to stand a statute requiring a claimant injured on municipal property to give timely notice of the injury to the mayor.[33] The general view of this section appears to be that it does not create rights but merely provides persons who have legal claims the right to bring those claims to court.[34] The court would then consider whether a precondition imposed on an individual before a case could be brought to court created an undue burden to the litigation of a claim.

Section 15: Unreasonable Search and Seizure Prohibited—Contents and Basis of Warrants

That the people shall be secure in their persons, papers, homes and effects, from unreasonable searches and seizures; and no warrant to search any place, or seize any person or thing, shall issue without describing the place to be searched, or the person or thing to be seized, as nearly as may be; nor without probably cause, supported by written oath or affirmation.

This section articulates the basic thrust of the U.S. Supreme Court interpretations regarding the U.S. Constitution's Fourth Amendment. The Missouri courts have stated that the state and national constitutional standards as to legality of arrest are not inconsistent.[35] In determining the issue of propriety of search and seizure, Missouri courts have followed closely the lead of national precedents and definitions.[36]

Section 16: Grand Juries—Composition—Jurisdiction to Convene—Powers

That a grand jury shall consist of twelve citizens, any nine of whom concurring may find an indictment or a true bill: Provided, that no grand jury shall be convened except upon an order of a judge of a court having the power to try and determine felonies; but when so assembled such grand jury shall have power to investigate and return indictments for all character and grades of crime; and that the power of grand juries to inquire into the willful misconduct in office of public officers, and to find indictments in connection therewith, shall never be suspended.

Section 16 is a very clear statement of the functions of grand juries, much more expansive and particular than that found in the national Constitution. The Missouri Supreme Court in 1977 did add a qualification to this section by stating that a grand jury cannot report its findings after investigation of a named public official except by indictment. If no indictment is found, the interim report should be expunged from the record.[37] The grand jury process is rather time-consuming and expensive and is seldom used in Missouri; however, it can play an important role in investigations of public officers. As a result, it provides an avenue for challenging governmental abuse.

Section 17: Indictments and Informations in Criminal Cases—Exceptions

That no person shall be prosecuted criminally for felony or misdemeanor otherwise than by indictment or information, which shall be concurrent remedies, but this shall not be applied to cases arising in the land or naval forces or in the militia when in actual service in time or war or public danger, nor to examination in any criminal case.

This is a clear statement of the use of indictment and information in the criminal process. In Missouri for most cases an "information" is used. "Information" is an accusation in the nature of an indictment from which it differs only in that it is being presented by a competent public officer (for example, a prosecuting attorney) rather than by a grand jury. When the use of an information was challenged as a violation of the Fifth and Fourteenth Amendments of the national Constitution, the Supreme Court of Missouri ruled that prosecution of felonies in state courts by information or indictment was not a violation of the national Constitution. Certiorari was denied by the U.S. Supreme Court, upholding the Missouri verdict.[38]

Section 18(a): Rights of Accused in Criminal Prosecutions

That in criminal prosecutions the accused shall have the right to appear and defend, in person and by counsel; to demand the nature and cause of the accusation; to meet the witnesses against him face to face; to have process to compel the attendance of witnesses in his behalf; and a speedy public trial by an impartial jury of the county.

This is a restatement of the rights of the accused as they exist under the national Constitution. An interesting question that has arisen recently is whether it would be possible to videotape the testimony of juveniles in child abuse cases to protect victims from the emotional stress of testifying before the accused. The Supreme Court of Missouri stated in a 1998 case that:

> Before video depositions of child victims of sexual abuse could be admitted at trial without violating the confrontation clauses of the Missouri and U.S. Constitutions, the state must produce evidence, at a hearing, sufficient to establish not merely that it would be less traumatic for the child to testify at an in-camera deposition, but that the emotional and psychological trauma which would result from testifying in open court or in the presence of the defendant in effect makes the child unavailable as a witness at the time of the trial.[39]

The Missouri court's interpretation of the accused's right to confrontation was affirmed by the national Supreme Court in 1990. In subsequent cases the Missouri Supreme Court has ruled that in regard to the accused's right to due process, in this case to meet the witnesses against him face-to-face, the Missouri Constitution was not more restrictive than the confrontation clause of the Sixth Amendment.[40]

Section 18(b): Depositions in Felony Cases

Upon a hearing and finding by the circuit court in any case wherein the accused is charged with a felony, that it is necessary to take the deposition of any witness within the state, other than defendant and spouse, in order to preserve the testimony, and on condition that the court make such orders as will fully protect the rights of personal confrontation and cross-examination of the witness by defendant, the state may take the deposition of such witness and either party may use the same at the trial, as in civil cases, provided there has been substantial compliance with such orders. The reasonable personal and traveling expenses of defendant and his counsel shall be paid by the state or country as provided by law.

Basically, this clause contains a restatement of the fundamental constitutional protections of the rights of personal confrontation and cross-examinations as interpreted by the federal courts. The goal is to maintain a fundamentally fair process in both criminal and civil cases. Note that the Missouri declaration of these rights is much more detailed than the national standards. In commenting on the guarantee of cross-examination, the state supreme court stated that under both the national and the Missouri constitutions the right of cross-examination is not without limitation. The right is sufficiently protected if the defendant has the opportunity to bring out matters as to the witness, poor eyesight of the witness, and even the very fact that the witness has a bad memory.[41]

Section 19: Self-incrimination and Double Jeopardy

That no person shall be compelled to testify against himself in a criminal cause, nor shall any person be put again in jeopardy of life or liberty for the same offense, after being once acquitted by a jury; but if the jury fail to render a verdict the court may, in its discretion, discharge the jury and commit or bail the prisoner for trial at the same or next term of court; and if judgment be arrested after a verdict of guilty on a defective indictment or information, or if judgment on a verdict of guilty be reversed for error in law, the prisoner may be tried anew on a proper indictment or information, or according to the law.

The self-incrimination clause was clarified by the Missouri court in 1979 when it stated that the provision that no person shall be compelled to testify against himself not only prohibited comments on the failure of a defendant to testify but also prohibited comments that would have the effect of compelling a defendant to testify.[42]

The double jeopardy provision repeats the protection included in the Fifth Amendment of the national Constitution. The Missouri Supreme Court has stated that there is "no readily discernible difference" between the double jeopardy guarantee of the federal provisions and Missouri's common law tradition.[43] However, if a jury cannot decide, the court may commit the defendant for a new trial. Also, if there has been an error in the trial procedure and the verdict is set aside, the court may again commit the defendant for a new trial if sufficient evidence of guilt was presented by the prosecution in the first trial.[44]

Section 20: Bail Guaranteed—Exceptions

That all persons shall be bailable by sufficient sureties, except for capital offenses, when the proof is evident or the presumption great.

This is basically the same constitutional provision adopted by the state of Connecticut in 1818. Since that time forty states have adopted substantially the same clause.[45] The Missouri courts have interpreted this to mean that the mere charge of a capital offense does not justify refusal of bail, and the state must bring forward evidence that would justify the denial of bail.[46]

Section 21: Excessive Bail and Fines—Cruel and Unusual Punishment

That excessive bail shall not be required, nor excessive fines imposed, nor cruel and unusual punishment inflicted.

These protections are also accorded under the national Constitution. The one that has caused some question in recent years is the cruel and unusual punishment clause as it applies to the death penalty. The Supreme Court of Missouri stated that the method of capital punishment used in Missouri did not constitute cruel and unusual punishment under the Eighth Amendment of the national Constitution. This position was also taken by the U.S. Supreme Court, though there is ongoing litigation to challenge the method.[47]

Section 22(a): Right of Trial by Jury—Qualification of Jurors—Two-thirds Verdict

That the right of trial by jury as heretofore enjoyed shall remain inviolate; provided that a jury for the trial of criminal and civil cases in courts not of record may consist of less than twelve citizens as may be prescribed by law, and a two-thirds majority of such number concurring may render a verdict in all civil cases; that in all civil cases in courts of record, three-fourths of the members of the jury concurring may render a verdict; and that in every criminal case any defendant may, with the assent of the court, waive a jury trial and submit the trial of such case to the court, whose finding shall have the force and effect of a verdict of a jury.

The provision dealing with courts not of record applies to divisions of the circuit court with jurisdiction over violations of municipal ordinances. Six-person juries can also be used in the associate circuit divisions if the parties consent.[48] The state supreme court also defined a trial by jury as something more than a trial by twelve persons; the term means a trial by twelve persons possessing proper qualifications for jury duty: impartiality between parties, living in the jurisdictional limit of the court, drawn and selected by impartial and disinterested officers, duly impaneled under the direction of a competent court, and sworn to render an impartial verdict according to the law and the evidence.[49] The court endorsed the power of a jury by ruling that the jurors had freedom to act in accordance with their own judgment.[50]

The Supreme Court of Missouri ruled in another case that a death sentence imposed by a judge did not violate a defendant's right to a jury trial. In a related case, the court ruled that no manifest injustice resulted from the prosecutor's inquiring of potential jurors whether they would be able to sign a death verdict if they were acting as foreman.[51]

The right to exclude potential jurors for cause was challenged as a denial of religious freedom in a 1995 case. The court ruled that excusing a potential juror on the basis that the individual could not follow the law because of a religious belief did not violate a protected religious freedom. The prospective juror had stated that he would exclude the death penalty even as a possibility since, according to his beliefs, only God gives life and therefore only God should take it.[52] Nor is it a violation of this section for a statute to assign determination of punishment to either judge or jury.[53] The right of a jury trial is generally understood to mean the defendant could waive a jury trial, but the Supreme Court of Missouri has held that there is no absolute right to waiver and that a defendant could waive the right only if the court approves.[54]

Section 22(b): Female Jurors—Optional Exemption

No citizen shall be disqualified from jury service because of sex, but the court shall excuse any woman who requests exemption therefrom before being sworn as a juror.

You might be surprised by this section since it seems to grant special rights to women, and indeed it does. But you might not be surprised to know that this section is no longer valid. The U.S. Supreme Court declared that authorizing women to request automatic exemption from jury service violated the "fair cross-section" requirements of the Sixth Amendment as applied to the states by the Fourteenth Amendment.[55] That is, a fair cross-examination of prospective jurors cannot deal with gender exclusively. Thus, to have women exclude themselves automatically excludes a section of the community from the jury pool.

Sections 14–22, then, deal with the basic protections of criminal procedure. They are crucial to a fair criminal justice system. It should be noted that criminal justice is an area that has been heavily influenced since the mid-twentieth century by the federal courts, though states like Missouri had court rulings defining rights in areas like the exclusionary rule and the right to counsel well before the national courts applied these protections to states.[56]

Section 23: Right to Keep and Bear Arms—Exception

That the right of every citizen to keep and bear arms in defense of his home, person and property, or when lawfully summoned in aid of the civil power, shall not be questioned; but this shall not justify the wearing of concealed weapons.

Although this section parallels, to some extent, the national Constitution's Second Amendment, it would appear to make a stronger statement for the right of individuals to keep and bear arms. The National Rifle Association would probably rate this as one of the more important sections of the Missouri Constitution. The Missouri courts have given great leeway to the legislature in defining this section by way of both limiting the right to bear arms and providing for concealed weapons. At first, state law prohibited the carrying of concealed weapons, and the courts upheld that limitation.[57] But when a statewide initiative allowing for concealed weapons under certain restrictions was defeated at the polls, legislators ignored this public decision and passed a law allowing for limited use of concealed weapons with permits gained after training. When this was challenged in the courts, the Supreme Court of Missouri interpreted Section 23 in such a way as to uphold that law. They said that the phrase "but this shall not justify the wearing of concealed weapons" did not prohibit the legislature's outlawing the use of concealed weapons but also indicated that the language did, indeed, allow the legislature to legalize concealed weapons if it chose. The language of the section was broad enough to allow the legislature to do what it willed in this matter.[58]

The court has, however, upheld limitations such as a law that makes it a felony to sell, transport, manufacture, or possess submachine guns. A machine gun is defined as any firearm that is capable of firing more than one shot automatically without manual reloading, by a single function of the trigger. Some exceptions are allowed for those licensed by the secretary of the treasury pursuant to the Gun Control Act of 1968, and for firearms defined as antique or collector's items. In some instances, the carrying of a deadly weapon in an open or concealed fashion is prohibited, and some places (churches, public meetings, and the like) can ban weapons, even concealed, by posting notices. An intoxicated person is forbidden to carry a deadly weapon as well. No person, sober or intoxicated, can exhibit a deadly weapon in a rude, angry, or threatening manner.[59]

Section 24: Subordination of Military to Civil Power—Quartering Soldiers

That the military shall be always in strict subordination to the civil power; that no soldier shall be quartered in any house without the consent of the owner in time of peace, nor in time of war, except as prescribed by law.

This section reflects a long-standing principle of American government and, to a certain extent, a recognition of the citizen's right to privacy. For example, in the U.S. Supreme Court's Griswold decision, the parallel Third Amendment (no quartering of troops) of the U.S. Constitution was cited as an indication of a privacy right that exists under the national Constitution.[60]

Section 25: Elections and Right of Suffrage

That all elections shall be free and open; and no power, civil or military, shall at any time interfere to prevent the free exercise of the right of suffrage.

This section is a clear statement of the importance of elections within the Missouri system. The Missouri Supreme Court did have a case based on this section that dealt with primary elections. In the primary a voter, by law, must state his party preference in order to receive a ballot in Missouri. This was challenged, and the court ruled that requiring a voter to state his preference was not a constitutional violation.[61]

Section 26: Compensation for Property Taken by Eminent Domain—
Condemnation Juries—Payment—Railroad Property

*That private property shall not be taken or damaged for public use without just
compensation. Such compensation shall be ascertained by a jury or board of
commissioners of not less than three freeholders, in such manner as may be provided
by law; and until the same shall be paid to the owner, or into court for the owner,
the property shall not be disturbed or the proprietary rights of the owner therein
divested. The fee of land taken for railroad purposes without consent of the owner
thereof shall remain in such owner subject to the use for which it is taken.*

Here is illustrated the importance Missouri attaches to the individual's
right to control his property. If private property is to be taken for public
purposes, the constitution requires that exact procedures be followed. It
provides a role for the judiciary to check for any possible abuses on the
part of the legislature, since condemnation is wholly a legislative power.
Or so the Missouri Supreme Court has ruled, saying that the power of
eminent domain does not depend on a specific grant in the constitution
but is inherent in sovereignty. Constitutional provisions relating thereto
are limitations on that power, not a granting of the power.[62] Since this is a
continuing and highly controversial power, there has been much legislation and litigation regarding eminent domain. Indeed, the federal courts
have recently given broad local powers in this realm.[63]

One area of confusion has been whether compensation is due to property owners when the value of the property is decreased by government
action.[64] Examples would be damage to land as a result of a condemnation
action and whether consequential damages may be recovered, even though
the taking of land was not a direct cause of damage.[65] In a relatively recent
case the Missouri court ruled that "when, as a result of a public works
project, private property is damaged by an unreasonable diversion of surface waters, whether by design or mistake, the owner may bring an action
for inverse condemnation." In a footnote to this case it was noted that even
a reasonable diversion of surface water by a public entity might constitute
a "taking." But since the case before the court was based on an unreasonable diversion, the court did not reach this constitutional point.[66]

You can see the complexity of cases dealing with the emotionally
charged governmental right of eminent domain and why limitations are
increasingly placed on its use by state constitutions and legislatures. For
example, due process requirements became part of the argument in a case
in 2008 when the court tried to define "just compensation."[67]

Section 27: Acquisition of Excess Property by Eminent Domain—
Disposition under Restrictions

*That in such manner and under such limitations as may be provided by law, the
state, and any county or city may acquire by eminent domain such property, or
rights in property, in excess of that actually to be occupied by the public improvement or used in connection therewith, as may be reasonably necessary to effectuate
the purposes intended, and may be vested with the fee simple title thereto, or the
control of the use thereof, and may sell such excess property with such restrictions
as shall be appropriate to preserve the improvements made.*

Note the detail of this section. The court has said about property rights,
"Generally speaking, a person is entitled to the exclusive control of his
property and the right to devote it to such uses as will best serve his
interest, but such rights are not absolute" because they must be balanced
against the needs of the whole community.[68] A recent example of this was
a case in which a city attempted to use its power of eminent domain to
condemn land beyond the city's boundaries on which a water reservoir
was to be built. Even though part of the land next to the reservoir was
to be used for a golf course, the state supreme court allowed the city the
use of this power, reasoning that the power was properly used to en-
hance the public interest.[69] The need for a safe public water supply and
for recreational facilities outweighed the owning farmer's attachment to
the property.

The use of property can be controlled as well as seized if there is a public
purpose. Thus, the taking of real property by a private corporation acting
pursuant to a city's redevelopment plan is defined as a public purpose.
Even before the federal courts got involved in this question, Missouri's
court accepted a legislative proposal under the process of eminent domain
for redevelopment purposes as conclusive evidence that the condemnation was public. The court stated that "once the legislative body finds an
area to be blighted, the taking of any tract of land included within the area
declared to be blighted is authorized as a taking for public use."[70] Thus,
the court legalized urban renewal programs in particular.

The U.S. Supreme Court in 2004 widened the use of eminent domain
for localities by stating well-maintained private homes could be taken by
localities. Missouri, like many states, responded to the public outcry at
this incursion by revising twenty-one sections of its statutes to restrict the
state from easy taking of private property.[71]

Section 28: Limitation on Taking of Private Property for Private Use—Exceptions—Public Use a Judicial Question

That private property shall not be taken for private use with or without compensation, unless by consent of the owner, except for private ways of necessity, and except for drains and ditches across the lands of others for agricultural and sanitary purposes, in the manner prescribed by law; and that when an attempt is made to take private property for a use alleged to be public, the question whether the contemplated use be public shall be judicially determined without regard to any legislative declaration that the use is public.

Still, there was more to say about limiting eminent domain. The major thrust of this section is the requirement that if a government is going to take private property, there must be a demonstration that this taking is necessary, and that adequate compensation is given for the property. The final determination of this will be made by the judiciary. Not only is fair compensation necessary, but the Missouri Supreme Court ruled that once a landowner is entitled to direct damages as a result of the loss of property, there are also consequential damages available if the value of the remaining land is reduced by being taken for public purposes.[72]

Section 29: Organized Labor and Collective Bargaining

That employees shall have the right to organize and to bargain collectively through representatives of their own choosing.

Although this section seems clear and inclusive, legislation was passed that excluded from collective bargaining public employees, including policemen, deputy sheriffs, highway patrolmen, national guardsmen, and teachers. Except for teachers, the excluded classes are made up of public safety officials. Whereas teachers are excluded from other broad areas of law (for example, special pension rights and certification procedures), a recent court case determined that teachers must be given the right to collectively bargain in Missouri.[73] However, school officials do not have to accept the demands of teacher groups but must honor any agreements made. Also the court has said that teachers do have limited rights, as well, in regards to positive actions to protect the agreements.[74] This 2007 case stated that this section applies to public employees as well as private-sector employees, leaving open the possibilities of further concessions to teacher groups.

Section 30: Treason—Attainder—Corruption of Blood and Forfeitures—Estate of Suicides—Death by Casualty

That treason against the state can consist only in levying war against it, or in adhering to its enemies, giving them aid and comfort; that no person can be convicted of treason, unless on the testimony of two witnesses to the same overt act, or on his confession in open court; that no person can be attainted of treason or felony by the General Assembly; that no conviction can work corruption of blood or forfeiture of estate; that the estates of such persons as may destroy their own lives shall descend or vest as in cases of natural death; and when any person shall be killed by casualty, there shall be no forfeiture by reason thereof.

This section closely follows Article III, Section 3, of the national Constitution in regards to restrictions on the legislature to designate or punish individuals for treason. Historically, this has been a means for political majorities to oppress their enemies, and democratic societies have tended to restrict access to this harsh accusation. Corruption of blood refers to the inability to disinherit blood relatives due to treason or suicide.

Section 31: Fines or Imprisonments Fixed by Administrative Agencies

That no law shall delegate to any commission, bureau, board or other administrative agency authority to make any rule fixing a fine or imprisonment as punishment for its violation.

This clause protects individuals by preventing government agencies from operating as judicial bodies in terms of punishments. The Supreme Court of Missouri has interpreted the term fines as used in this section to refer to the type of fine that could be imposed in lieu of imprisonment.[75] Thus, the definitions of fine, as it is used in this section, would be a monetary punishment imposed for the commission of a crime or misdemeanor.[76] Bureaucracies are forbidden to use this device on their own.

Section 32: Crime Victims' Rights

1. *Crime victims, as defined by law, shall have the following rights, as defined by law:*
    (1) *The right to be present at all criminal justice proceedings at which the defendant has such right, including juvenile proceedings where the offense would have been a felony if committed by an adult;*

(2) *Upon request of the victim, the right to be informed of and heard at guilty pleas, bail hearings, sentencings, probation revocation hearings, and parole hearings, unless in the determination of the court the interests of justice require otherwise;*

(3) *The right to be informed of trials and preliminary hearings;*

(4) *The right to restitution, which shall be enforceable in the same manner as any other civil cause of action, or as otherwise provided by law;*

(5) *The right to the speedy disposition and appellate review of their cases, provided that nothing in this subdivision shall prevent the defendant from having sufficient time to prepare his defense;*

(6) *The right to reasonable protection from the defendant or any person acting on behalf of the defendant;*

(7) *The right to information concerning the escape of an accused from custody or confinement, the defendant's release and scheduling of the defendant's release from incarceration; and*

(8) *The right to information about how the criminal justice system works, the rights and the availability of services, and upon request of the victim the right to information about the crime.*

2. *Notwithstanding section 20 of article I of this Constitution, upon a showing that the defendant poses a danger to a crime victim, the community, or any other person, the court may deny bail or may impose special conditions which the defendant and surety must guarantee.*

3. *Nothing in this section shall be construed as creating a cause of action for money damages against the state, a county, a municipality, or any of the agencies, instrumentalities, or employees provided that the General Assembly may, by statutory enactment, reverse, modify, or supersede any judicial decision or rule arising from any cause of action brought pursuant to this section.*

4. *Nothing in this section shall be construed to authorize a court to set aside or to void a finding of guilt, or an acceptance of a plea of guilty in any criminal case.*

5. *The general assembly shall have power to enforce this section by appropriate legislation.*

This section was inserted by an overwhelming public vote of more than six to one in the fall of 1992 as a response to political concerns about rising crime rates. It reflects a desire for more fairness in the treatment of victims and defendants by the criminal justice system. Basically, in reading the many provisions of the section, it tries to allow for victims of crimes to be informed at every step in the criminal justice process against the person who harmed them and to give them protection from that person by information and by police action if necessary. It also provides for the ability to give some input in some instances, and it sets up the ability of the legislature to provide for restitution to victims. Restitution in the form of monetary compensation has been minimized by the limited availability of moneys for this purpose. The section does protect the state from suit by victims, however.

Section 33: Marriage, Validity, and Recognition

That to be valid and recognized in the state, a marriage shall exist only between a man and a woman.

This section was a constitutional amendment added in August 2004. It clearly defines marriage exclusively as being between a man and a woman and not including same-sex unions. This is a continuing controversy that the U.S. Supreme Court will no doubt have to settle eventually. The courts have tended to use the equal protection clause for cases like this, though some think it should be considered under the federal Constitution's "privileges and immunities" section.

Section 34: That English Shall Be the Language of All Official Proceedings in This State

Official proceedings shall be limited to any meeting of a public governmental body at which any public business is discussed, decided, or public policy formulated, whether such meeting is conducted in person or by means of communication equipment, including, but not limited to, conference call, video conference, Internet chat, or Internet message board. The term "official proceeding" shall not include an informal gathering of members of a public governmental body for ministerial or social purposes, but the term shall include a public vote of all or a majority of the members of a public governmental body, by electronic communication or any other means, conducted in lieu of holding an official proceeding with the members of the public governmental body gathered at one location in order to conduct public business.

This amendment was put on the ballot by vote of the legislature in 2008. Note that the wording is specific and reads like a statute rather than an amendment. Indeed, opponents in the approval election pointed out that a Missouri statute, added in 1998, already stated that English was the "common" language of Missouri. In addition, the law says that Missouri recognizes that "fluency in English is necessary for full integration" into American society. The supporters of the English-only movement argued that a non-English-speaking public meeting would confuse the majority. The amendment passed with 83 percent of the vote. Several states have adopted this policy either within their constitutions or as statutory law.

In summary, what is apparent from examining closely the Missouri Bill of Rights is that the framers of the 1945 constitution, and those of earlier constitutions, followed the American tradition of placing limitations on governmental power, particularly when government interacts with individuals. Amendments since 1945 have strengthened this tradition. The Missouri Bill of Rights appears to provide a solid foundation for the continued protection of individual rights against undue government actions.

Article II: Distribution of Powers

This one-paragraph article is designed as an introduction to the presentation of the Madisonian model of government as reflected in its Missouri form. This is particularly reflected in the provisions outlining the three branches of government with specific powers and a system of checks and balances.

If the first and paramount importance of the Missouri Constitution is to impose limitations and restrictions on the exercise of state power, Article II fulfills this function by dividing power into three distinct departments: legislative, executive, and judicial. The theoretical justification for the concept of separation of powers is that it is a guarantee against too much power in any one government department. In so doing, it fulfills the Madisonian model by protecting the people from a concentration of power that might endanger their rights, even their freedom.[77]

Section 1: Three Departments of Government— Separation of Powers

The Powers of government shall be divided into three distinct departments—the legislative, executive and judicial—each of which shall be confined to a separate magistracy, and no person, or collection of persons, charged with the exercise of powers properly belonging to one of those departments, shall exercise any power properly belonging to either of the others, except in the instances in this constitution expressly directed or permitted.

Even though the basis for separation of powers is the dividing of power into three mutually exclusive departments, it has never been feasible in practice to adhere absolutely to this principle. It would be impossible to have a complete separation of powers. Thus, there are a number of areas where exceptions must be made. The major role of the judiciary in this regard has been to safeguard the separation while allowing the exceptions necessary for government to function.[78]

The condition under which legislatures may delegate some rule-making authority to executive agencies has been a difficult problem for the courts at both the national and the state levels. The basic position taken by the Missouri courts is that executive officers may not be permitted to make and promulgate rules that are strictly and exclusively legislative. The Missouri General Assembly, however, has established a sufficiently definite policy that authorizes administrative officers to make rules, regulations, or orders relating to administration or enforcement of laws.[79]

Separation of powers is designed to maintain the independence of each department, while at the same time recognizing that there are no absolute lines of demarcation between functions. For example, it is a legislative power to prescribe a general rule, and it is a judicial power to decide upon the rights of the parties under the prescribed rule.[80]

The Supreme Court of Missouri has ruled that the right of the court to pass judgment on the constitutionality of a law enacted by the General Assembly and signed by the governor is a proper judicial function under the Missouri Constitution. The court rejected the argument that to allow the court this right would be a violation of the separation of powers provision of the constitution.[81]

The state legislature may, in spite of the separation of powers, delegate legislative power to local governments. The delegation of these powers to local governments is held to be very different from delegating power to a statewide executive agency.[82] Without this decision, the state legislature would be involved in every city and county ordinance in the state—which is clearly impractical.

The state supreme court has also allowed some flexibility in the interrelationship among the various branches of local governments. For example, the removal of a city court judge by a mayor was ruled not to violate the separation of powers principle. The court viewed in this specific case the removal of the judge as dealing with the judge's tenure and not the function of the judiciary.[83]

In summary, the separation of powers doctrine, as outlined in Article II, ensures that power is not centralized in any branch; however, the distinctions among functions of branches are not always clear, nor is it useful or logical in all instances to have absolute separation. How to maintain the separation of powers, while at the same time allowing government to function in a fair, efficient, and rational manner, is a major challenge for the three branches of government. In the end, of course, it is politics and judicial interpretation that determine where the lines of demarcation are pragmatically drawn.

3

The Legislature

This is the first of three chapters exploring the branches of government as they are defined and operate in Missouri. The method will consist of an introductory essay at the beginning of each chapter on the branch being discussed. This introduction will give an overview of the structure and operation of the chapter's branch of government. Following that, the text will again turn to an analysis of the actual sections of the article in some detail and in order, continuing the dual nature of these chapters. The close-consideration section of the chapters will not provide the actual wording of the constitution, as was a necessity for the Bill of Rights chapter. The Missouri Constitution is so specific in these areas that to quote all sections would double the size of the text unnecessarily.

Unlike the previous chapter on the Bill of Rights, which, of necessity, focused on the limitations of government in a very specific and technical arena of constitutional protections, the material covered by these chapters deals with the political system as it operates through the three branches of government and as grounded in constitutional operational principles.

Legislative Functions

State legislatures perform a variety of functions, some of which are obvious and some of which are not so apparent to the casual observer. These functions are not significantly different from the functions performed by the national legislature; they simply have a different environment within which to operate and a different scale of operation. State legislatures have fewer members than the national legislature, shorter sessions (at least most do, including Missouri), more constraints on actions (particularly the need for a balanced budget), and somewhat less public scrutiny, all of which produces a different dynamics to the politics of the state legislature.

Legislatures have three fundamental functions: public policy making, legislative oversight, and representation. As we briefly discuss each of these functions, you will notice that some of what the legislature does is what we expect them to do from the very definition of their role. Other things they do are not so obvious and give insight into the conflicts inherent in the process that individual legislators face in making decisions. Some of these functions are extraconstitutional but vital to the understanding of the role of the legislature in state government.

Public Policy Making

This is the central role of the legislature. Our system of government, founded upon the liberal philosophies of John Locke, Rousseau, and other Enlightenment thinkers and made pragmatic by the American founding fathers, sees the legislature as the dominant element of government. If we are to have government by the consent of the governed (the central tenet of democracy), then those who represent the governed most directly must have the dominant responsibility for governing. That, of course, is the legislature, as we have already seen through court interpretation of the Missouri Bill of Rights. Governing consists first and foremost of making policies concerning the entire community that makes up the political unit—the definition of public policy.

Making public policy consists of three basic activities: making laws, establishing and defining state governmental activities, and accumulating and appropriating the funds to carry out these activities. First, then, legislatures must set the legal foundations and rules that not only refine the operations and structure of government outlined in the constitution but produce the specific mechanisms to carry out the functions of government outlined in the constitution. Then they must produce projects and programs that respond to the demands and needs of the public at any particular time. Bureaucracies, broadly provided by the constitution, are specified and refined by law. Goals of the constitution as defined by contemporary politics are pursued by legislation—whether these are economic, social, or ethical goals or goals in the area of defining criminal justice. Legislation, then, is passed to provide for infrastructures (roads), social supports (health, unemployment, recreation), and safety (criminal justice system, workplace safety). In addition, the state must provide the underlying legal basis for the legitimate relationships between individuals and between individuals and the state: civil law.

Fundamentally, legislation can be divided into criminal law, civil law, and operational legislation. *Criminal law* is that set of legislative acts that produce and sustain the criminal justice system. These laws define the parameters of acceptable individual behavior in relationship to the health and safety of the community as a whole. All societies set fundamentally the same laws dealing with physical harm to others, protection of property, and honest and fair interactions in the economic and social arenas within the community. In short, these laws limit the actions of individuals and are defined by the relationship between the individual and the state or relationships that the state defines as fair or proper relationships between individuals. The idea is that the state acts first and foremost so that individuals cannot act on their own when they are or are perceived to be threatened or harmed by others. Criminal law produces a legal relationship of individual and the state through legal cases involving individuals accused of violations by the state, after police action, being taken to trial, and if found guilty punished. Cases under criminal law are denoted by *Missouri v. "John Doe."* Thus, the state is officially accusing an individual of a crime under legislation passed by the state. Most criminal law is passed and defined by the state legislature, but some misdemeanor law (minor violations like traffic laws) are left to localities by the constitution.

Civil law is the body of legislation set up to regulate the relationships between individuals in the community. This area of law covers a broad spectrum of public disputes between individuals. These are most notable in the areas of commercial interactions (contract law, business law), social relationships (marriage, juvenile custody), and defining ownership (probate, real estate deeds). Laws define the parameters of relationships in these areas and means to protect individual interests when challenged by other individuals. They allow for protections of individuals by way of civil suits against other individuals who violate their economic or social interests. State law is primary in setting these relationship patterns; federal laws can rarely intercede. The case foundations for conflicts under civil law, then, are denoted by *John Doe v. Jane Doe* or *John Doe v. Ajax Corporation*. Note that corporation entities are treated as individuals under civil as well as criminal law.

Our purpose here is not to describe these complex areas of law in any detail, only to illustrate the point that the fundamental role of legislatures is to make laws that regulate the society and that laws fall into a variety of categories.

The third important area of legislative responsibility is the defining of and providing resources for the *operational* aspects of government. What we mean by this is the ability of the legislature to establish activities and programs that provide resources and services to the citizens of the state. The specific areas of operation will be defined more particularly in the chapter on the executive, but we need to make it clear at this juncture that much of the year-to-year activity of the state legislature and its budget process is focused on operational programs and services. These range from support for infrastructures of the state (roads, bridges, buildings) and providing for an educational system (public schools and higher education institutions) to providing citizen support in the areas of health, welfare, unemployment, and recreation, among other areas.

All of this operational activity must be paid for, of course, and thus it is that a major portion of the time and attention of the legislature is devoted to raising taxes and appropriating resources. The annual budget process takes up a good percentage of legislative time and energy because everything that state government does must be officially authorized and then paid for (appropriated) by the legislature.

Legislative Oversight

The second major function of the legislature is oversight. This means that the legislature, largely through its committee structure, is responsible for checking to see if the laws and moneys that it promulgates are being administered by the executive branch in a manner conducive to the intent of the legislature. Only in this way can there be a legislative check on the appropriate spending of the state's resources and the efficient management of the state's affairs. A further source of this function will be found in the state auditor's office, described in the executive article.

There are four means of oversight used by the legislature: committee review of bureaucratic actions, postaudit reviews, casework, and use of sunset laws.

Committee review of the actions of the various bureaucracies of the executive provides a continuity of communication and interaction between the two branches of government. The legislature operates through committees organized around subject areas, as we shall discuss shortly. Bureaucracies are organized by subject responsibilities as well, making it easy to match the two, thus allowing committees to review the operations of the bureaucracies within the areas with which they are most familiar. This provides not only a check on the executive but more positively a flow of information on the viability and utility of legislation in areas both entities are responsible for. If laws or programs are not working well, this can be discovered by committee oversight. If they are working well and could benefit from added legislation or moneys, this too can be transmitted within the committee oversight process.

Postaudit reviews. Just as committees can review and examine the work of the bureaucracies in their area of concern, so too must committees review the spending of their appropriations by the bureaucracies. By scrutinizing the audit reports of and through hearings on the various agencies of government, the committees can examine how the moneys appropriated have been spent and if they have been spent in the areas intended. Postaudit reviews can give the legislature an insight into the effectiveness of programs and institutions that they finance. In this the legislature has the help of professionals on their legislative staff and to some extent from the state auditor's office.

Casework. All legislators hear from their constituents on a fairly consistent basis. When that communication takes the form of a question or problem with government, the legislator (or a staff member) logs that into their office system as a "case" to be dealt with. Taking care of constituents is an extraconstitutional (political) part of the responsibly of the legislator. Some spend a good portion of their time and attention on this activity because of the individual needs reflected by the requests but also because each case dealt with successfully can rebound into votes in the next election.

Increasingly, programs and operations of government are complex and confusing. When individuals find that government has either not responded appropriately to their needs or failed to perform a responsibility related to the individual, then an outlet for solving the problem often is communication to their local legislator. The legislator will try to deal with the problem by answering the individual if they have knowledge that deals with the complaint or by passing the complaint or inquiry along to the appropriate government office or agency.

Casework benefits both the constituent (when it works) and the legislator. But if the legislator and his colleagues get several complaints about the same program, law, or agency, then they get an idea that something needs fixing. This is what makes casework such an effective oversight tool for the legislature.

Simply put, *sunset laws* are pieces of legislation that are passed with an expiration date—the sun will set on them. These can be any type of legislation but most likely will be legislation that sets up, or expands the responsibilities of, programs or agencies. This is used as a means to force a reevaluation of either an experimental or a controversial program or law.

Sunset laws can be effective legislative as well as political tools. States often are in the forefront in trying new approaches to problems. Experiments can be hidden disasters if they are not reviewed to examine their effectiveness. Sunset laws force the legislature to revisit many new or experimental approaches to contemporary problems. In addition, it is not unusual to find a controversial program or law given a sunset date as a compromise aimed at getting the necessary votes to enact it. These hard-to-pass pieces of legislation may get by those legislators on the fence if they believe they are not making the legislation permanent. A sunset provision allows them to revote on the measure at a date in the future, evaluating the outcome of its operation.

Representation

Each legislator must, either consciously or unconsciously, decide two fundamental questions as he or she approaches the job: who do I represent and how do I represent them? This is another extraconstitutional role in many respects but a vital part of the definitional role of legislator.

The first question seems to have a deceptively easy answer; each legislator has a definite *geographic district* containing their legally defined constituents. They most definitely are charged with representing them in their respective house of the legislature. But often the legislator is called upon more informally, though often insistently, to represent groups outside their districts that perceive them to have a responsibility for their interests. These often come from various social sectors of the citizenry of the state.

Most common of these sectors are those with a perceived *sociological connection* to the legislator. We mean by this groups that identify with the legislator because of who that legislator fundamentally is in terms of race, religion, ethnic identification, or gender. It is simply true that if you are an African American legislator in Missouri, you may well be perceived by African Americans throughout the state to represent them on those issues perceived to be related to this segment of the population. Though most African American legislators in Missouri have come from Kansas City or St. Louis, they find a constituency throughout the state on many issues.

In an age when social issues take center stage—topics like abortion, school choice, or prayer in school—certain religious groups look to fellow communicants in the legislature for support for their views on these issues whether they are geographic constituents or not. This can be a benefit or a complication for the legislator, depending on their response to these external pressures. Who do I represent? It can get complex if you are a Catholic legislator from a Protestant district, for example.

Gender issues find women legislators asked to respond not just as legislators from a specific geographic area but as women. A variety of issues have periodically been described as "women's issues." How do female legislators respond to interest groups of women who expect them to respond to legislative decisions as women regardless of the profile of their districts? Legislation that deals with protection of children is a graphic example. Then again, many legislators find support even for their reelection from groups outside their districts because they are women, or Fundamentalists, or African American. You get the idea.

Last, there are *economic constituencies* that transcend district boundaries. Why do we often see representatives in the legislature from various professions or from labor backgrounds asked to comment on legislation affecting those economic interests? We expect to see lawyers in office, but why identify insurance agents, farmers, retired teachers, or health professionals? Obviously, from a general perspective, they are citizens and equally likely to be civic minded and active in the political community. But in the context of our discussion you might see that often they are sponsored by or encouraged to run by either their employers or members of their industry or profession.

Since the state regulates many industries, it is not surprising that these industries would like to have "insiders" representing their point of view to their fellow legislators. To have an insurance agent on the committee dealing with legislation in this area is to have positive representation. Teachers on education committees, farmers on agriculture committees—the list can get longer, but the point is clear. People in the legislature in particular economic interest areas are bound to be seen by, if not even sponsored by, groups and people throughout the state who look to them for specific interest representation. Here again, this can be a blessing or a curse depending on the issue, the individual, the geographic constituency, and the perception of fellow legislators. Many legislators appreciate the expertise of fellow legislators in areas they are not familiar with. Others may feel undue influence in symbiotic relationships between legislator and interest group.

There are often, then, many influences on legislators as to whom they represent. Not the least influence, of course, is legislators' own perception as to how they should represent. There are two polar options with many gradations in between. On one pole is the perception that the representative is a *trustee*. This is an indication that the legislator believes that the constituents were exposed to the views, platform, and performance of the legislator as a candidate for office and they agreed enough to elect him or her. The trustee then perceives the legislative decision-making role as that of exercising good judgment on the issues before the legislature. After all, the constituents knew the legislator and his or her views and thus sent him or her to exercise good judgment on behalf of these constituents. The legislator feels responsible, but relatively independent.

On the other pole, the opposite perception is that of the *delegate*. This legislator believes that the constituents sent him or her to reflect their interests as closely and completely as possible. This legislator is to vote the way he or she perceives the majority of his or her constituents wants. A representative is to reflect the views of those represented in a very specific way regardless of the opinion or evaluation of the legislator on any particular piece of legislation.

The problem is, of course, that representatives cannot adhere strictly to either polar approach because of the complexity of their situation. To be a complete trustee is to lose the next election because you inevitably will ignore some explicitly popular positions in favor of your view of a rational decision. This will get you bounced. If you are a complete delegate, you will find yourself in a muddle when it comes to voting on issues that there is no clear indication of what your constituents feel on that issue. This is the case not only on closely contested viewpoints but also on the myriad of bills, amendments, and items you must approve or disapprove in the legislative process that your constituents simply do not know or may not care anything about. For example, in a state like Missouri, split between large urban areas and a significant rural and farm constituency, what happens in the inevitable situation in which there is an agriculture bill before the legislators from urban areas, or urban legislation that rural legislators must vote upon? Most constituents in these differing areas simply have no view on those contrasting issues. This may leave the legislator free to vote as a trustee or to "trade" votes with their urban or rural kin.

The bottom line is that most legislators find their role to be somewhere toward the middle of the two approaches—leaning usually toward one pole or the other, but certainly not purely trustee or purely delegate. Constituents should be able to determine which way their legislator leans, however, by observing him or her closely.

Fundamentals of the Missouri Legislature

States differ widely in the way in which their legislatures are set up. Scholars tend to use a broad division to describe the fundamental operational assumptions of state constitutions. They postulate three types: full-time legislatures, part-time legislatures, and those in between. Basically, they categorize states by the criteria of whether they run their sessions virtually the whole year (like the federal legislature), whether their salaries are relatively high or low, and whether the legislators have large or small staffs. Not surprisingly, the first type of state tends to be dominated by the larger states—California, Illinois, New York, Pennsylvania. They are the ones with large and diverse populations—urban, suburban, and rural—and thus with complex needs.

The third type contains largely the smaller, more homogeneous states— Utah, Vermont, Wyoming, Idaho, Maine, North Dakota. Fewer total resources and fewer needs limit the legislative agenda. The in-between type, not surprisingly, holds close to half of the states, including Missouri.

The first thing to know about the Missouri legislature is that it is called the General Assembly (GA), divided into two houses, the House of Representatives and the Senate. House members have two-year terms, and Senate members have four-year terms. Term limits have been passed in the state, which means that a member can serve only eight years in each house—though they can go to the other house for another eight years if they can get elected. By constitutional limitation, the legislature meets from the beginning of January to the end of May each year. Indeed, legislation can be voted upon only until the middle of May, and the rest of the month is for administrative cleaning up of the session.

Like the national example, the formal sessions are numbered by the two-year term of the session coinciding with the terms of the members of the House of Representatives. All legislative activity must be completed within the two-year cycle or start over again the next term after the election of a "new" legislature.

Missouri pays its legislators nearly thirty-two thousand dollars a year (2008) plus a per diem for each day the legislature is in session to compensate for food and housing expenses while away from home. As for staffing, each member of the House gets a secretary and a full-time assistant; a senator gets an additional assistant given the larger districts. Some use leftover campaign funds to hire additional help. Interns help with the load as well. They all have access to a common pool of staff in each house that can help with research and bill writing, depending on their assignment by the leadership of each house.

Interestingly, there is no correlation between fitting into one of these three types and the actual size of the legislative bodies. California, our largest state, for example, has a legislature that ties for thirty-fifth in a rank order of total size. New Hampshire, thanks to a House of 400 members, ranks number one. Missouri has a relatively large legislature ranking seventh amongst the fifty states, with 197 combined members.

Just as interesting, there is also no correlation between the sizes of the two houses of the legislatures in the states. New Hampshire's Senate, for example, is only 34 strong. Missouri illustrates the imbalance often seen between the two houses: its Senate has 34 (one of the smaller) members, its House of Representatives 163 members (one of the larger). Thus, it takes only 18 votes to pass or stop a bill in the Senate, making each senator regardless of political party of great importance on every bill. To the contrary, a member of the House is not necessarily needed on any piece of legislation because he or she is only one of 163 (82 are needed for passage).

You might notice that this reflects heavily and often quite dramatically upon the potential unity of political party actions in the respective houses. Party discipline plays a much more dynamic role in the House, where the vote's crucial political capital is watered down, but each vote is needed in the Senate, giving the senator a crucial power position. A Republican senator can vote against his leadership and gain displeasure, but since he or she may be desperately needed on the next vote, the approbation is not severe nor can it last long. As we shall note later, this accrues to the committees even more specifically, given the smaller committee numbers in the Senate and the larger ones in the House.

What are the demographics of the General Assembly? Women made up around 22 percent of state legislators in 2008 nationwide. Missouri had in its Ninety-fourth General Assembly (2007–2008) 38 women, 31 in the House and 7 in the Senate—19.3 percent, down a little from 21.3 percent in 2004. Women tend to be Democratic representatives by a two-to-one margin over Republicans. The broad trend toward more women in the legislature comes fairly late, since the first woman elected to the Missouri Senate, Mary Gant, was not elected until 1972, joined by Gwen Giles in 1977 as the first African American woman. It was not until 1960 that the first African American male, Theodore McNeal, joined the Senate. About 8 percent of national legislators are African American; they constitute 9 percent (2007) of Missouri's legislature, 17 in the House and 3 in the Senate.

Since the 2001 elections both houses of the Missouri legislature have been controlled by Republican majorities, reversing a fifty-year period of control by the Democrats. Overall, Missouri's numbers are typical given that they are near the national average of the percentage of women and African Americans in the legislature.

Legislative Leadership

Though only partially outlined in the constitution, understanding leadership roles in state legislatures is crucial to understanding the making of public policy. Given the short legislative sessions and the fact that the lawmakers must deal with an average of fifteen to seventeen hundred bills and resolutions during the session, organization and direction are needed if the business of the legislature is to get done. At the beginning of each two-year numbered session, leadership is chosen for that session. The House and Senate leadership can both be summarized by identifying first formal leadership and then informal leadership.

By *formal leadership* we mean officeholders who are selected by all members of each house as the recognized officers in the workings of its business. In the House of Representatives the central leader is the Speaker of the House, chosen by majority vote of all 163 members. This means, of course, that whichever party has a majority in the House will choose its leader as the Speaker, since in this instance, at the very least, the party members virtually always vote unanimously. To allow for continuity a Speaker pro tem (a substitute whenever the Speaker is unavailable) is also elected and filled by the majority-party candidate—in essence the number-two party leadership.

The speakership is a powerful role, often said to be second only in influence to the governor. He or she appoints the chairs of all committees, assigns each House member to committees, assigns bills to committees, regulates the schedule of legislation that comes from committees for consideration on the House floor, and heavily influences the flow of debate by setting the rules by which bills are considered on the House floor. Often the fate of legislation is greatly in the hands of the Speaker (aided by his party leadership team), especially for fiscal bills that must originate in the House.

Formally, the chairs of each of the committees of the House are also in this category of leadership, though the Speaker chooses these chairs and, indeed, may remove them if they prove uncooperative with the Speaker's agenda. Since the committees are all populated with a balance roughly equal to the party balance in the House, there is virtually always a chair from the majority party enjoying a majority on his or her committee from their party. In this instance, it does not guarantee straight party-line voting in committees since there is not strict party discipline available, but the chair has significant influence on committee members (even those in the minority party), as they largely control the agenda of the committee (in consultation with the Speaker).

The Senate has as its formal leader, by constitution, the lieutenant governor. He or she presides over the Senate whenever they please—though they rarely please to do so. Their only powers are to recognize speakers in turn and to vote in case of a tie. Because senators can rise and speak for as long as they wish under their open-debate rules, the first power is negligible and the second occurs only infrequently. Indeed, it is not unusual for senators to manipulate close votes to keep the lieutenant governor from voting. The branches of government are jealous of each other, and the Senate hates to have legislation determined by an executive officer. Therefore, only when it is clear that the Senate is split evenly or there is a media event will the lieutenant governor appear in the chair.

This leaves the effective formal leader of the Senate the President Pro Tem of the Senate. This post is the equivalent in power to the Speaker in the House, with much the same influence over scheduling legislation, committee assignments, and timing of floor deliberations. But because there are only 34 senators, making each senator's vote a crucial one, these tools of discipline are not as effective as they are for the Speaker of the House. To be one of 163 means you need at least some patronage of the leadership to be effective; thus, you try not to make too many waves. The Speaker and chairs have many weapons to affect the individual representative's agenda. This is not so much the case in the Senate, given its size and its more open-debate format. By that is meant the assumption that each senator can speak on the floor (and in committees) on any issue for as long as they care to. Although filibusters are sparsely used, the threat of holding up legislation (given, again, the short sessions) can give senators leverage, especially toward the end of the session. Still, the president pro tem and the chairs of committees who make up the formal leadership of the Senate have significant powers.

The *informal leadership* in the legislature is composed of those elected by the caucuses of the respective parties in each house. The Democrats and Republicans in each house, separately, convene before the beginning of the session and choose their leadership—sort of like superclubs organized within the legislature. Each house has a majority leader and a minority leader along with a bevy of other "club" officers. In each instance, the majority floor leader is actually the number-two or -three leader of the majority party (formal leaders being the top leadership). They direct the caucuses and orchestrate the floor leadership (debate plans and execution and political maneuvering) of those bills designated with party positions. The House needs more caucus officers to manage its larger numbers, so its members elect an assistant majority floor leader, whips (assistants to the two floor leaders), a caucus chair and secretary, and a variety of other roles geared toward maximizing party actions in the House and to spread leadership among the varied segments of the party in the House.

The party with a minority of members in the House elects its own caucus leadership that parallel that of the majority: a minority floor leader with an assistant and whips as well as a caucus chair and secretary. If the minority party were to win the majority in the next election, then the minority floor leader would more than likely be chosen the Speaker of the House, meaning that this role is the central leadership role of the minority.

The Senate follows the same pattern of informal leadership, with majority and minority leaders, assistants, whips, caucus chairs, and secretaries. Again, given the size differential, Senate party leadership and unity are not as effective on a consistent basis as is the House leadership. Much, of course, depends on the personality and leadership skills of the individuals filling all the leadership roles. Some of these generalizations, then, will not prove true for any particular time or circumstance.

Committee System

Like all American legislative systems, Missouri's legislature does business largely through the committee system. Work is divided by issue area, and the committees of the two houses review legislation based on their assigned topic areas. Legislatures work on the basis of a division of labor that is structured in a committee system. Bills are matched to committees that are organized to deal with the subject matter of common areas of legislation. The assumption is that over time the members of each committee gain some experience with and expertise in the broad subject area concerned. Often it means that members are assigned to committees whose subject matter they are already familiar with, either through personal interest, experience, or occupation. The characteristics of the legislator's district also will play a role—for example, urban members will serve on urban-oriented committees.

Because it has more members to assign to committee work, the House has more committees than the Senate. Also pushing up the committee work of the House is their responsibility to put together the budget and initiate the appropriations bills. Thus, during the Ninety-fourth General Assembly (2007–2008), the House had eighteen standing (permanent) committees plus six appropriations committees. It is interesting to note that from time to time new leadership will reorganize the committee system by lowering or raising the number of committees and shuffling their titles (and thus responsibilities). In the Ninety-second General Assembly, for example, there were twenty-eight standing committees and six appropriations committees. This would seem to hurt special interests that look to the state legislature for help. After all, the state regulates many industries and provides a great deal of financial and legal support to several areas of citizen life. To make up for the consolidation of standing committees, the House leadership has created twenty-five special committees that focus on overall public policy in specific areas of concern. For example, though the Small Business Standing Committee was folded into another committee, there is a Small Business Special Committee. Other topics cover urban issues, agribusiness, family services, immigration, utilities, senior citizens—the list is long. The special committees placate the special interests by doing research and focus hearings on the subjects while not unduly bogging down the legislative process.

The six appropriations committees take the general spending guidelines provided by the work of the Budget Committee and put them into specific dollar amounts to appropriate to specific purposes and agencies. Since everything government does has to be paid for, much of the politics of the Missouri legislature is embodied in the work of these committees. And, of course, the chairs of these committees wield extraordinary influence, though always under the general guidance of the Speaker. The very names of these appropriations committees indicate where Missouri spends the bulk of its moneys: Agriculture and Natural Resources; Education; General Administration; Health, Mental Health, and Social Services; Public Safety and Corrections; and Transportation and Economic Development. The first fourteen bills enumerated by the House process are always the appropriations bills.

The Senate has only sixteen committees, all of which together must cover the same spread of legislative subjects and close to the number of bills covered by the House committees. For example, there is only one Appropriations Committee that must review all the appropriations bills that come out of the six House committees. Topics must be consolidated in forming the Senate committees if the thirty-four members are to be able to staff all the committees without undue scheduling problems. For example, one committee deals with economic development, tourism, and local government while another covers agriculture, conservation, parks, and natural resources. Senators must be particularly adept at multitasking; they average four standing committee assignments plus varied other duties. This load resulted in the fact that the Senate in the Ninety-fourth General Assembly had no special committees. In contrast, a House member will generally be on two standing committees and perhaps one or two special committees or other assignments.

That does not mean that the Senate does not cater to special interests in doing its business. The Senate simply uses more particularly a third category of committees to perform a dual task for them. These are the joint committees, often noted as statutory committees because they have members from both houses and thus need a statute to establish their legitimacy. There are a series of fifteen joint committees set up with membership from both houses that tend to deal with specific contemporary problems or issues (for example, court automation, corrections, gaming and wagering, and transportation oversight). Some cover specific areas that the House also deals with by means of the special committees—homeland security, economic development, tax policy, government accountability. Some of these joint committees are under sunset provisions.

Committees do the research and the legal background searches on bills as well as vet the political conflicts attendant to the bill. The committee is responsible for filtering the workload, since all seventeen hundred or so bills put in play cannot be fully dealt with—nor, given the duplication and frivolity of many bills, should they be dealt with. This legislative process creates increasingly difficult work given the many contentious issues in today's politics and the increased specialization and technicality of much legislation.

The Legislative Process

The constitution of Missouri gives the legislature the ability to order its business as it wills, so the following process is set up by the legislature for itself, not the constitution. You know the old saw, there are two things you don't want to know—how they make sausage and how they make laws. Unfortunately, too many citizens have no idea about the complexity of the lawmaking process, and too many dismiss the process as somehow corrupt. The reality is that legislators contend with a wide range of pressures and counterpressures. Reference the discussion above on the functions of the legislature. Besides the formalities of the processes we outlined, there are a fountain of informal political pressures that come from party leadership, interest groups, contributors to legislators' campaigns, and individual citizens (often with heartbreaking problems). It simply is not easy grinding all of these ingredients into a good legislative product.

Legislative bills must start somewhere; someone must write them. In point of fact, anyone can write a bill, and there are many sources for those bills. Executive offices must carry out legislation and thus know how present laws and programs are working or not working. Their suggestions for new legislation or new programs or changes to old ones often find their way into a bill presented to a legislator for action. Interest groups may write a bill, as may individual citizens. Even legislators get into the act of producing a bill from scratch occasionally. The point is that anyone may write a bill, but only a member of the legislature can introduce a bill into their respective house.

However a bill comes to the legislator, the first thing she often does is send it to that house's legislative staff to be put into legal terminology that fits the topic and intent of the bill. Once the bill is in good form, the legislator is ready to file it, to put it into the "hopper," the term used for submission of the bill. Enterprising legislators may try to coordinate efforts with a member of the other house by having that member put the same bill into their hopper, hoping to shorten the time traveled by the bill.

Once in the process, a bill follows fundamentally the same route in each house. So as we briefly describe this process, keep in mind that the bill has to repeat each step in each house to become law.

A bill can be prefiled in Missouri starting December 1 of each year. Since the legislature starts in early January, there is already a backlog of bills to put into the system. The *first step* in the process then is simply having a legislator file (submit) the bill. The *second step* is to have the bill "read" two times as a means of formally putting it into the system. The bill waits in line and is taken up by the house and "read" a first time: its first reading. The full bill is not read; that would take too much floor time. At this step the bill simply is given a number and a formal title. In the House the number will be preceded by an *H*, in the Senate by a *S*. Thus, the designation would look like: HB 126, "A Bill to Reform the Corrections System," or SB 65, "The Education Reform Bill of 2008." If in the form of a resolution, the bill has no formal consequence except giving the sense of the legislature and is designated as *HR* or *SR*.

After the first reading, the bill gets back in line again until taken up for a second reading. This seems routine, but politics plays a role even this early. It is the Speaker of the House or the President Pro Tem of the Senate that directs the timing of the second reading and then performs the important task of the reading—assigning the bill to a committee. This may sound unimportant, but it is often an important decision point for the bill. Many bills could be sent to one of two or three committees because their subject matter overlaps these committees. The leadership knows the composition of all the committees and their chairs and can help or hurt the prospects of a bill, depending upon what committee to which the bill is sent. The second reading can make or break a bill's prospects from the outset.

The *third step* in the bill's sojourn through the process is the early committee actions, usually public hearings. The chair of the committee is crucial here: he or she usually has the end ability to either take up the bill or not. Note that if the chair decides not to take up the bill, the bill simply lays there and dies if not revived later. If the chair decides the committee should deal with the bill, the chair can decide the order in which the bill will be taken up. Remember, bills continue to come into the committee, and the order they are taken up, if they are at all, can determine whether the bill has the time to get through the whole two-house process in the short time the legislature is in session.

If and when taken up, and the bill is one of some substance, the committee will hold public hearings on it. The chair, another of his perquisites, invites the people who will present evidence and viewpoints pro and con on the bill. In this way a legislative record is built with data and evidence to support and oppose the bill. It is this material that follows the bill throughout the rest of the process. Usually, the bill's sponsor is first to testify, and then others are invited as the chair deems necessary. Committee members nominate speakers; interest groups and individuals vie for a forum before the committee, but the chair orchestrates the whole procedure.

Once the hearings are over (or if a noncontroversial bill is taken up without a hearing), the committee goes into executive sessions to discuss the disposition of the bill—the *fourth step*. It is here that most of the hard work is done on the bill. The committee scrutinizes all aspects and wording of the bill and must make decisions on it all. The committee may do what it pleases with the bill: it can amend it, combine it with a similar bill, slice it up, rewrite portions of it, even redo it to the point where its sponsor disavows it. If the latter happens and the committee approves the bill, it becomes the "committee substitute bill." In the end the committee either votes against the bill, effectively killing it, or votes for the bill: designating it as "Do Not Pass" or "Do Pass," the latter sending it along to the floor of the house.

Since committees constitute a small percentage of the number in the full house, the bill depends on the vote of a minority of the full representatives to send it along or to kill it. Given the significantly small numbers in the Senate, a relative few votes determine the fate of the bill in their committees. Even in the House where the committees are larger, the relative number of votes needed to control the bill is small. This is why the committees are the focus of most of the political pushing and pulling in the Missouri legislature. Here is where lobbyists and other interest activities focus. This may well be the most significant decision point in the legislative process. It is true that one-third of the members of the full house the bill is going through can overturn a vote if that committee has voted "Do Not Pass" and bring it to the floor anyway, but this rarely happens.

The *fifth step* in the process is the consideration of the bill by the full body on the floor of the House or Senate. This is called in Missouri and most states the "perfection" of the bill. If it passes here, it is done so in its final or perfected form. This, of course, is another key decision point for the bill. Since all of the committees are sending bills to the floor of the respective houses, flow must be managed, and it is here where the Speaker and President Pro Tem have the exercise of important powers. There is a Rules Committee in the House of Representatives that puts on the procedural "rules" by which each bill will be taken up. This means it tells (1) when the bill will be taken up by the full house, (2) if and for how long there will be debate, and (3) if and under what conditions amendments will be allowed. The Rules Committee is guided by the heavy hand of the Speaker in these matters. The bill can be fast-tracked by putting it in the front of the line, or it can be delayed, often for long periods, by keeping it at the end of the line of pending bills. It can even be put below the batches of bills that come in after it.

Debate on the House floor can be important, for it allows representatives to have a record of their support or opposition, and it allows for the airing of interest positions on the bill. Noncontroversial bills do not need much debate, whereas more substantive or complex bills may need significant periods of debate. Within this process, amendments may be crucial in determining whether enough votes can be gathered to pass (or to kill) the bill. The Rules Committee can put a particular limit on the number of amendments allowed to be voted upon, or it can put a specific time limit on the passing of amendments. The politics of the scramble for amendments on many pieces of legislation can be quite competitive—even brutal. After all, if my bill needs an amendment to attract a segment of the legislators who say they will vote for the bill if certain changes are made, and the Rules Committee says no amendments, the bill is lost for want of a small change. On such turns the fate of much legislation.

In the Senate there is no comparable rules committee. The leadership, headed by the president pro tem, determines the rules by which each bill is to be considered. But then the basic processes of the Senate differ, since its rules allow for open debate. This means that any senator may rise and speak on a bill for as long as he or she wishes and offer amendments at will. Only a closure vote of two-thirds of the members can shut off debate and lead to an immediate vote on a bill. A filibuster, then, is possible in the Senate to delay or defeat a bill. After all, there is a lineup of bills trying to be passed, and senators who sponsor or support those bills want to make sure there is time to pass those bills through the process. Delay may mean defeat for them. Then again, any senator who filibusters must take into consideration the enmity of those senators if they proceed. So you must fervently believe in your filibuster's purpose, or have significant help of other senators, if you do not want to suffer down the road for your actions.

Once the debate and amendment process is complete in each house, there is an up-or-down vote on the bill. But that does not end the floor consideration of the bill. If the bill passes, it is referred to the printing office to be put in permanent type with all changes so that there is a formal and final form of the bill in print. This allows for the legislators to see exactly what the perfected bill looks like when approved. This sets up the *sixth step* in the process, which is the third reading of the bill. Simply put, the bill comes before the house for a final vote on the printed version of the bill, which, of course, has already received a positive vote. The full house votes again on the bill, but almost always it receives the same majority vote to pass as it did before.

This final passing of the bill allows it to be sent to the other house to go about the approval (or not) process through the same steps. This simple transfer is the *seventh step* in the process. If the other house passes the bill, there are three options. First, if the bill is basically in the same form except for minor changes, the leadership of the two houses will meet and reconcile their differences and have both house floors pass the bill again. If, however, there are substantive changes in the bill by the second house, a *conference committee* will be formed to negotiate compromises to put the bill in one form. This committee consists of equal members from each house (routinely three or four) and works on majority vote. The committee members in this role represent their respective houses, not their other constituencies. That is to say, conference committees represent more or less exclusively the feelings of their house on each bill. The reality, then, is that the members from each house tend to vote as a bloc on the compromises. They check often with their leadership and the floor leader for that bill to make sure the compromises they agree to are acceptable to the voting majority on that bill. Late in sessions bills could die for lack of agreement on a compromise if time runs out.

If and when the conference committee finds agreement, the bill is sent back to each house for what is almost always a pro forma *final floor vote.* It is an up-or-down vote since continued tampering with bills would make it impossible for the legislature to get a lot done. Of course, once passed, the bill goes to the *governor,* who can sign or veto the bill.

The legislature can *override* a veto with a two-thirds vote of each house. If the governor vetoes the bill while the legislature is in session, the legislature can then vote to override. If the veto comes after adjournment, the constitution directs a veto session in September of each year specifically to give the legislature the opportunity to overturn the veto. Missouri's legislature has historically failed to overturn more than just a handful of gubernatorial vetoes. All legislation passed goes into effect on August 28 unless the legislature by three-fifths vote directs the immediate application of the legislation.

Throughout this whole process politics plays a significant role in what happens—politics of interest group influence, political party coherence, leadership effectiveness, and legislator response to their various constituencies. This is the people's business, and it should be expected that a complex society would provide a complex of influences on its public policy decisions.

Article III:
The Legislative Department in the Constitution

This article provides the basic guidelines for legislative activity in the state. Its fifty-three sections are divided into four parts. Sections 1–20 focus on the rules for the General Assembly. Sections 21–35 concentrate on legislative proceedings and detail the requirements of the legislative process. Sections 36–48 outline the limitations on legislative power, focusing specifically on financial limitations. Finally, Sections 49–53 deal with the initiative and referendum process for making public policy. Unlike the previous article discussion, we will not quote each section but describe their key elements and say what the courts have had to say about certain elements of the article.

Sections 1–20: Rules for the General Assembly

The Missouri General Assembly is the principal institution for developing public policy for the state. Some matters of state policy are, indeed, settled by use of constitutional amendments or popular initiative and vote; however, it is out of the question to think that continuity of state business can be sustained in this manner. The General Assembly, the combined legislature, is the one body that meets regularly to make public policy through a process of political interplay and studied deliberation.

Section 1 of Article III, then, states that the legislative power shall be vested in a Senate and a House of Representatives to be styled "The General Assembly of the State of Missouri." The key term here is vested. The General Assembly has all legislative power not granted elsewhere, prohibited by the national Constitution, or expressly or implicitly withheld by the Missouri Constitution. There is, however, no comprehensive enumeration of the power of the GA, maximizing its flexibility. Except for the restrictions noted, the power of the state legislature is unlimited and practically absolute.[1]

After the broad statement regarding the power of the General Assembly, the remainder of Article III provides much detail pertaining to the granted and withheld powers and activities of the GA. The procedure for electing members to the GA is covered in several sections. Section 1 requires that there be a reapportionment of senatorial and house districts after each decennial census to equalize the number of people in each district. In a special election in 1966, voters approved an amendment that provided for the method that is detailed in Sections 2 and 7 of this article. The core of the procedure is the appointment of a commission to draw the reapportionment plan. Major political parties must have equal representation on the commission, creating difficulties in finding a majority since reapportionment is a very partisan process. It is very difficult to get Democrats and Republicans to agree upon drawing of lines in an equitable manner; each wants lines protecting districts with historical majorities of their adherents. If the commission becomes deadlocked (which happened in 1991), the second method provided is to convene a substitute commission of six judges from the courts of appeals appointed by the state supreme court. A majority of these judges then decide upon a new reapportionment plan. Either of these commissions must, of course, follow the U.S. Supreme Court requirements that districts be contiguous, compact, and their populations as nearly equal as possible.[2]

Procedures for House (Section 2) and Senate (Section 7) districts are basically the same. Probably given the controversial nature of the process, the sections provide that reapportionment is not subject to referendum. Also, members of the apportionment committee cannot run for the General Assembly for four years following institution of their plan. Still, the actual operation of the apportionment procedure usually results in the bipartisan commission's being stalemated. This means the judges usually draw up the final operational plan.[3]

Qualifications for state representatives and senators are provided in Sections 4–6. Each representative shall be twenty-four years of age and must have been a qualified voter for two years and a resident of the district he is chosen from for one year (Section 4). The House has 163 districts, the Senate 34. A senator shall be thirty years old, a qualified voter for three years, and a resident of the district for one year. The minimum age requirement for the House was upheld against an equal protections challenge in the state supreme court. The court ruled that the age requirement was rationally related to the state's legitimate interest in ensuring mature and experienced legislators.[4]

These qualifications are not of much concern, although on occasion the residency requirement of a member is challenged. The legislative body of which the person is a member has exclusive right to determine whether the member is qualified to hold or assume office, and courts are without jurisdiction to determine the issue of removal based on residence.[5] The requirement of residency has been challenged, but the state supreme court found that the equal protection clause of the U.S. Fourteenth Amendment did not eliminate the right of the state of Missouri to establish and enforce the one-year district residency as a prerequisite to serving as a state legislator.[6]

Other requirements concerning members of the General Assembly are as follows. First, members cannot hold any other lucrative office or employment under the United States, the State of Missouri, or any municipality. Second, if members of the GA change their residence from the district from which they were elected, the office must be vacated. And third, all members of the GA must take the following oath: "I do solemnly swear, or affirm, that I will support the Constitution of the United States and of the state of Missouri, and faithfully perform the duties of my office and that I will not knowingly receive, directly or indirectly, any money or other valuable thing for the performance or non-performance of any act or duty pertaining to my office, other than the compensation allowed by law" (Section 15). Any member refusing to take this oath would be deemed to have vacated the office, and any member convicted of having violated this oath would be disqualified from holding any office of trust or profit in the state government.

An additional restriction concerning members of the GA was adopted by voters in the general election of 1992. This section provided for term limitations for members of the GA. No person may serve more than eight years in either the House of Representatives or the Senate or a total of sixteen years in both houses. Term limitations were also passed for members of the U.S. Congress from Missouri (Section 45a), restricting Missouri's senators to two terms and representatives to four terms. However, this amendment will not go into effect until one-half of the states have enacted term limits on their members of Congress. This may conflict with the U.S. Constitution, for the U.S. Supreme Court in a 1995 case declared that states could not add qualifications for membership to Congress.[7] Still, this provision also states that the wish of the citizens of Missouri is to have their federal representatives voluntarily follow the term limits in this section. None have so far.

Other sections in this category deal with some rather miscellaneous issues, including: (1) a provision providing for compensation, mileage, and expenses of GA members (the GA by law sets these amounts periodically); 2) a limitation on the number of legislative employees (again, set by the GA by legislation); 3) a requirement that each house appoint its own officers, be sole judge of the qualifications and elections of its own members, determine the rules of its own proceedings subject to the constitution, punish members for disorderly conduct, and only with the concurrence of two-thirds of all members expel a member; and 4) a provision that in all cases except treason, felony, or breach of the peace, members are privileged from arrest during the session of the GA and during the fifteen days preceding and following the session. In addition, members are exempt from question about any statement on the floor of either house, in committee, or in committee reports. This last protects the members from libel charges. Clearly, the legislators are to be in charge of their own business procedures and protected from outside legal pressures.

The article limits the time the legislature can be in session. This is common for most state legislatures and seems to arise from a desire to compel legislators to perform their work with dispatch and without undue time to produce poor legislation. States want to minimize overlegislation generally. It is believed that with less time available, subjects of major importance and the budget will absorb the interest of legislators and tend to crowd out trivial matters or matters of merely personal or local interest. In addition, shorter sessions might capture public attention more readily and make public service in the legislature more attractive to persons of ability. For whatever reason, Missourians seem to prefer the shorter sessions. As late as 1988 Missourians voted on an amendment to shorten the amount of time the legislature spent in session, putting it at its present length, and it passed by an overwhelming majority—1,421,973 to 406,250.

This amendment (Section 20) provides that the GA shall begin meeting on the first Wednesday after the first Monday in January and adjourn the session at midnight on May 30. It also provides that all bills in either house remaining on the calendar after 6:00 p.m. on the first Friday following the second Monday in May are tabled. The time in between these two dates is to be devoted to the enrolling, engrossing, and signing (in open session by officers of the respective houses) of bills already passed before the 6:00 p.m. deadline. Clearly, all effective legislative activity ends in the middle of May. The GA prior to this had a short session in even years (January to April) and a long session in odd years (January to June 15). In addition, the GA used to consider bills up until midnight of the last day of the session, which gave rise to an impression (not unwarranted) of much wheeling and dealing, with legislators voting on bills that they were not properly prepared to consider. The amendment modulated this problem, but did not eliminate it.

Another 1988 change (now Section 20b) provides for the calling of a special session by the GA. A petition, stating the purpose for which the session is to be called and signed by three-fourths of the members of each house, would convene the GA into special session. Prior to this change, only the governor could call for a special session, a power he or she retains. The time limit for a special session is set at thirty days, and it may only consider matters that are specifically contained in the petition or governor's call. No appropriations bill may be considered in the special session if in that year the GA has not passed the operating budget of the state. Special sessions are often called directly after the scheduled veto session since legislators will already be in Jefferson City.

Sections 21–35: Legislative Proceedings

The constitutional limitations on legislative procedure and the form in which bills are passed are designed to secure reasonable and transparent deliberation. In addition, they are aimed at ensuring, to some degree, a sense of responsibility on the part of lawmakers. These restrictions are contained in Sections 21–35.

Section 21 provides for the style of the state laws. Each law must begin, "Be it enacted by the General Assembly of Missouri, as follows." The section requires that no law shall be passed except by bill, and no bill shall be amended in its passage through either house so as to change its original purpose, though this provision is often stretched to its limits. Bills may originate in either house, but money bills traditionally start in the House.

Every bill must be referred to a committee of the house in which it is pending (Section 22). One-third of the members of the house considering the bill may remove a bill from a committee and place it on the calendar for consideration of the full house. In each house, records of proceedings must be maintained; these will include the recorded votes of the members of the committees filing reports (passing) on bills. If committees meet outside of the legislative session time, each house can establish rules by which they operate.

Sections 21 and 22 deal with procedure and format, and have generated little controversy or challenge. Section 23, however, has produced major conflicts. It states, "No bill shall contain more than one subject which shall be clearly expressed in its title, except bills enacted under the third exception in Section 37 of this article and general appropriation bills, which may embrace the various subjects and accounts for which moneys are appropriated." A great many bills over the years have appeared to violate this provision. The court interpretation of this provision is that the controlling test for determining whether a statute contains more than one subject is whether all provisions of the statute fairly relate to the same subject, have a natural connection to it, or are the incident or the means to accomplish its purpose.[8] This clause is to help legislators and the public recognize the purpose of legislation and to prevent the practice common in legislatures (for example, Congress) of allowing so many additions to bills that they become unrecognizable as the original bill or embody confusing numbers of issues. Combining issues or confusing the bill's intent makes it hard for legislators to determine whether to vote for the bill if they do not approve of every topic it contains. Extraneous provisions in bills can sneak unpopular or special interest material into an otherwise clean bill. Obviously, even with the court definition, the application of this section is difficult to interpret or police in practice.

Section 24 states that no bill may be considered for final passage in either house until it has been printed and copies have been distributed to all members, necessitating the second vote on the floor of each house after the third reading. There must be a final printed form for legislators to be assured of what the bill does.

There is also a limitation on the introduction of bills (amended, again, in 1988) (Section 25). Appropriations bills cannot be taken up for consideration after 6:00 p.m. on the first Friday following the first Monday in May of each year. This responds to the change in session timing and ensures that appropriations bills will receive early consideration by the GA and not be a result of the chaotic closing day of the session of the legislature. The section also requires that no bill other than an appropriations bill may be put in the hopper in either house after the sixtieth legislative day unless introduction is consented to by a majority of the members of each house or the governor requests consideration by a special message.

The recording of votes in each house is considered in Section 26. Each house must keep a journal of its proceedings including a yea or nay vote if requested by five members. The journal will contain all votes yea and nay as well as abstentions. There must be a public record.

Section 27 demands an absolute majority vote in each house floor for passage of legislation. This means that to pass a measure in the House there must be eighty-two affirmative votes and in the Senate eighteen.

Methods for reviving, reenacting, and amending bills are detailed in Section 28. The thrust is to ensure that there will be a complete record of changes that are made in the proposed bill.

The effective date of laws is provided for in Section 29. Except for appropriations, laws passed by the legislature go into effect ninety days after adjournment of the session in which they are enacted. If the GA feels there is an emergency need for the bill, it can by a two-thirds vote direct that the bill take effect immediately upon the governor's signature.

Section 30 outlines the finalizing of legislation by stipulating the signature of the presiding officer in open session. Objections to the legislation may be made by a member, but these are simply sent to the governor for his consideration.

Signatures send the bill to the governor, whose responsibility is outlined in Section 31. He has fifteen days to consider it; if signed, it becomes law. Within the fifteen days he may veto it by sending it back to the originating house. Once the legislature has adjourned, however, the governor has forty-five days to decide whether to sign or veto the bill. If there is not action by the governor within these time periods, the bill becomes law without his signature.

Overriding a veto is provided for by Section 32. It takes a two-thirds vote of both houses. If the veto comes after the session ends, the GA automatically reconvenes on the first Wednesday following the second Monday in September to consider an override, called a veto session.

Section 33 was repealed in 1986. Several items of purely organizational impact are included in Sections 34 and 35. All general laws are to be revised at least every ten years, and a permanent joint committee on legislative research is mandated, performing duties assigned to it by the GA. This becomes the major resource for legislators, giving them the ability to employ staff who can provide valuable services in bill drafting and fiscal analysis. At one time this was the only staff available to legislators, but now each has at least minimal help.

Sections 36–38: Limitations on Legislative Power

Limitations on the financial powers of the Missouri General Assembly are listed in Sections 36–38 of Article III and in Article X. The first deals with the payment of state revenues and receipts to the treasury and limitations of withdrawals to appropriations, and it provides an order of priorities that the GA must follow in the appropriations of money. This has never been an important aspect of the constitution since the legislature has always been able to fund all the categories, but it is a good illustration of the thrust of the constitution in regard to limitations on legislative powers. The order of appropriations must be as follows: (1) payment of sinking fund and interest on outstanding obligations of the state (debt); (2) money for public education; (3) payment of the cost of assessing and collecting the revenue; (4) payment of the civil lists (state employees); (5) support of charity and other state institutions; (6) money for public health and welfare; (7) all other state purposes; (8) the expenses of the General Assembly.

Limitations on state debts and borrowing are contained in Section 37. The basic thrust is to limit the amount of money the state may borrow and to determine the period that will be allowed for repayment. If the state wants to borrow more than one million dollars, the GA or an initiative would have to submit the amount, purpose, and terms of the debt to a vote of the people. Unlike the federal Constitution, Missouri limits drastically the ability of the state to borrow money for operating budgets.

The remaining parts of Section 37 (a–f) list the state's obligations regarding proposals approved by the people: (a) consists of the authorization, interest rate, and payment requirements for a state building bond issue; (b) provides for water pollution control funds (adopted in 1971); (c) provides for some additional water pollution control bonds (adopted in 1979); (d) provides for state building bonds (adopted in 1982); (e) provides more bonds for water pollution control, improvements of drinking water systems, and storm water control (adopted in 1988); and (f) provides for the issuance of bonds to provide funds for rebuilding buildings at higher-education institutions, corrections, and youth services (adopted in 1994). Note the specificity of these areas that read like statutes rather than parts of the state constitution; this is one of the reasons the constitution is so long.

The article continues (Section 38[a]) by giving specific directions to the legislature in terms of restrictions on the use of state funds and credit. Basically, it prohibits the GA from using public money, property, or credit to assist any private person, association, or corporation except for aid in a public calamity and for general laws providing pensions for old-age assistance, aid to dependent children, aid to the blind, or for discharged members of the armed forces and persons in need of rehabilitation.

Section 38(b) provides for the GA to levy an annual property tax of between one-half and three cents on one hundred dollars of valuation for a pension for the deserving blind.

Then Section 38(c) provides for neighborhood improvement districts and authorizes cities and counties to create these districts, though it limits the total indebtedness for such districts.

The listing of financial restrictions on the GA continues in Section 39, adding a provision that forbids the GA from removing the seat of government from the City of Jefferson. Then Section 39 (a–c) provides very specific requirements dealing with the authorization of bingo, the state lottery, and pari-mutuel wagering. Furthermore (d) was added in 1992 to ensure that all state revenue derived from the conduct of all gaming operations would be appropriated solely for the public institutions of elementary, secondary, and higher education. Authorization for riverboat gambling on the Missouri and Mississippi was added by yet another amendment in 1994. As times change and cultural values evolve, the constitution must be changed to reflect the political reflections of the citizens as they evolve.

It should be noted here that limitations on the legislative power of the GA continue in Article X (taxation), which defines the state's taxing power and places a number of additional limitations on legislative power. These will be considered in chapter 7.

Sections 39–48: Special, Local, and Private Laws

The theme of limitations of powers continues as the article provides restrictions on the GA's ability by limiting the enactment of special, local, or private laws. These are laws that apply to, or are for the benefit of, some particular person, corporation, or locality; or are not of general and uniform application throughout the state; or do not apply to all persons or corporations included in some authorization classification. This provision is supposed to prevent favoritism, corruption, and legislative consideration of petty matters. It does not fully accomplish this, of course, since legislation often is carefully worded to sound general but is applicable only to a specific target.

Still, the constitution (in Section 40) deals with the prohibition of passing any local or special law by the GA and contains a list of thirty specific restrictions. You can reference the constitution for the list; it is enough to indicate the care the constitution takes in this regard. The general distinction is that a statute referring to persons or things as a class is a general law, whereas a statute relating to particular persons or things is special legislation. Examples of prohibited local and special laws are the granting of specific divorces; remitting of fines, penalties, and forfeitures or refunds legally paid into the treasury; changing the law of descent or succession; changing the names of persons or places; and the incorporation of specific cities, towns, and villages or changing their charters by state law. General laws must cover all these instances. Note that, for example, the state law defines how to incorporate a city or county, but the GA cannot do this for one specific city or county.

A fairly recent example of the application of this restriction was the state supreme court's decision that set aside a law that dealt specifically with one company. The court declared this to be special legislation and, therefore, unconstitutional.[9] In another case, an environmental regulation was held to be invalid since it imposed sanctions on only a few companies and did not treat similarly situated companies performing identical acts. The regulation was ruled unconstitutional since it violated the special law provisions, and it was also viewed as a bill of attainder.[10] A bill passed by the GA that provided for licensing of excursion gambling boats was declared to be a special law. The legislation designated the area by geographical locale and by precise size and type of boat.[11] It is an example of how the legislature manipulates wording to direct laws to specific corporations.

Sections 41 and 42 provide additional restrictions on the use of local and special laws. The GA is prohibited from enacting a special or local law by the partial repeal of a general law, and if such a law is being considered (and does not clash with other restrictions), the locality must be given thirty days' notice prior to its introduction. The restriction against the enactment of special laws applies with equal force to municipalities.[12]

These restrictions still leave the legislature with considerable latitude, and it appears that local and special laws continue to exist.[13] The GA finds that, on occasion, the passing of such laws through clever wording and insinuation allows it to further its agenda, and the courts have found it difficult to curb this activity. As several recent cases demonstrate, the court continues to define what actions violate this provision.[14]

Further provisions of Article III prohibit the GA from interfering with the disposal of land by the national government (Section 43). This section also states that no tax may be imposed on federal land, nor can tax rates imposed on lands owned by people residing outside the state be different from those by people residing within the state.

Section 44 says that no law can fix rates of interest for any particular group or class engaged in lending money; it is a uniform interest rate provision.

Section 45 deals with reapportionment of congressional district boundaries, noting that the districts must be "composed of contiguous territory as compact and as nearly equal in population as may be." A continuing problem with the combined responsibilities assigned for this task to both governor and GA is that if these two are controlled by competing parties, a GA redistricting can be vetoed by the governor. In this case, like state reapportionment, a three-judge panel will redraw the districts.[15] Then Section 45(a) defines the attempt to establish congressional term limits that we described above in relation to the GA term limits.

Section 46 commits the GA to provide for the organization, equipment, regulations, and functions of an adequate state militia. It goes on in 46(a) to define the emergency duties and powers of the GA in the event of an enemy attack. The GA may convene immediately and provide for emergency succession of powers and duties and continuity of governmental operation.

Finishing these miscellaneous descriptions of the powers of the GA, Sections 47–48 deal with the GA's abilities for acquisition and paying for state parks, monuments, or artifacts of its history.

Sections 49–53: Initiative and Referendum

The initiative and the referendum are both examples of legislation by the citizenry. Initiative refers to the initiation of legislation or constitutional amendments by the public. Referendum refers to the vote of the electorate on these matters (we shall cover the amendment process originating with the GA later). When these modes of "direct legislation" are combined in an initiative and referendum package, the final decision as to what shall or shall not become law is taken away from the legislature and reserved for the electorate. Although the great mass of legislation is enacted by the legislature, the use of the initiative and referendum has meant that the electorate has deemed it necessary to settle some public issues. In addition, the initiative and referendum provide the public with a check over the activities of the General Assembly.

Simply put: "The people reserve the power to propose and enact or reject laws and amendments to the constitution by the initiative, independent of the General Assembly and also reserve power to approve or reject by referendum any act of the General Assembly" (Section 49). The procedures for doing so begin in Section 50. If a constitutional amendment is proposed, initiative petitions must be signed by 8 percent of the legal voters in two-thirds of the U.S. congressional districts (thus presently six of the nine). If a law is proposed, initiative petitions must be signed by 5 percent of the legal voters in two-thirds of the congressional districts. Note that a legal voter is defined as a registered voter, not just someone qualified to vote.[16] Both proposed amendments and proposed laws must include only one subject and be in proper form.

In a 1991 case the Supreme Court of Missouri voided a statute that required that sample initiative petitions be submitted to the secretary of state one year before the initiative would be placed before the voters. This requirement was ruled to interfere with the people's right to use the initiative. As a result of this decision, initiative petitions may be presented to the secretary of state anytime during periods between general elections.[17]

An interesting provision in Section 51 states that if there are conflicting measures approved at the same election, the one receiving the largest affirmative vote shall prevail. This section also provides that the initiative may not be used for the appropriation of money other than for new revenues created by the initiative. The initiative takes effect when approved by a simple majority of the votes cast.

The procedure for use of the referendum is outlined in Section 52(a). Any bill passed by the GA, except emergency measures and appropriations bills, may be placed on the ballot either by the General Assembly or by 5 percent of the legal voters in two-thirds of the congressional districts. If the bill is approved by the referendum, it becomes law. The governor cannot veto a bill passed by referendum.[18]

The basis for the number of signatures required on initiative petitions for amendments and initiative petitions for proposed laws and referendums is explained in Section 53. The total vote for governor at the general election prior to the filing of the petitions is used to determine the number of signatures of legal voters necessary on petitions. Thus, if a congressional district cast two hundred thousand votes for governor, an initiative petition for amendments would need sixteen thousand signatures, and initiative petitions on laws or referendums would need ten thousand.

The general thrust of the constitutional provisions of Article III, "Legislative Department," is to regulate quite specifically many areas of legislative activity. The result is a General Assembly that is far weaker in terms of its control over public policy for its jurisdiction than the national Congress for its areas of responsibility. It would appear that even though in theory the Missouri GA is closer to the people and thus, in theory, more responsible to them, this does not inspire more trust for legislative discretion. It should be noted that despite these limitations, the legislature has enormous input into the standards of conduct in the state. For example, the legislature can by statute state that life begins at conception and that an "unborn child" is a person. This was done in an involuntary manslaughter statute, and the Supreme Court of Missouri sustained this definition by affirming a conviction of an individual charged with causing the death of an unborn child.[19]

Therefore, despite the fact that the Missouri General Assembly plays an exceedingly important role in state government, it appears to be viewed by the constitution as a more or less necessary political process, which ought to be, nevertheless, systematically curbed and checked. Throughout Article III are provisions that, combined with Article X's limitations and the governor's veto ability, operate to place substantial limitations on the exercise of legislative power. This reflects the fundamental philosophical foundation of our system of government—the limitation on the powers of the operating organization of government.

4

The Executive Department

State executive departments differ significantly from the federal executive in basic ways. First, all states directly elect more than one executive, and, second, the constitutions of states have the tendency to specifically outline the structure of the executive. Most states separately elect by statewide ballot four to eight executives. These executives have separate constitutional authority over the branch of the executive that they head and thus are not responsible to the governor. This is in stark contrast to the president of the United States, who is the sole elected executive for the national government. The only "exception" to this statement is the concurrently elected, on the same ballot, vice president. This leaves the vice president as a mere appendage of the presidency; a spare in case of the death or disability of the president, if you will.

Missouri has a separately elected governor and lieutenant governor plus the four offices most separately elected in American states: secretary of state, treasurer, auditor, and attorney general. The reader will readily appreciate that since each of these is elected on their own, the electorate may well choose to put into the executive representatives of both of the major political parties. Even the governor and lieutenant governor may well be, and in recent decades often have been, of separate political parties. More often than not, Missouri voters have kept a balance of party adherents among their six elected executives. Historically, these have been highly contested offices because they can be stepping-stones to either the governorship or the U.S. Senate. Since the institution of term limits for state legislators, these offices have become even more desirable.

The second contrast between the national and the Missouri executives is the fact that the Missouri executive bureaucracy is extensively outlined and defined directly within the constitution. The U.S. Constitution says precious little about the structure and organization of the bureaucracy of the executive. It leaves all of this up to the legislature. Although many details are left to the legislature in the Missouri Constitution, one of the reasons the constitution is so long is because each of the administrative departments of government bureaucracy is defined and empowered, some at length, within the constitution. It should be noted that not all states include this extensive description of the executive organization within their constitutions. Many follow the federal lead and let the legislature define the bureaucratic needs and organization of the executive bureaucracy to fit the needs of the times. They are content to let the constitution simply define the statewide elected executives.

In describing the Missouri executive, then, this chapter will discuss the formal and informal roles that the governor plays and the roles of the other elected executives and briefly describe the constitutional departments of the bureaucracy. Then the chapter will follow the pattern of the text and specifically describe the executive department as outlined in the constitution.

The governor, as chief executives at all levels, must perform a variety of roles, both constitutional and extraconstitutional. Those roles can be classified into two basic streams: the fundamental role as chief of state and the variety of roles under the general thrust of the governor as chief of government.

Chief of State

As chief of state the governor is the ultimate representative of all of the citizens of the state. This is a nonpolitical role that focuses on ceremonial and representative activities. Whenever there is the necessity for government to reflect the feelings and sentiments of the entire citizenry, the governor tends to be the voice to transmit them. Ceremonial occasions are many and cover the spectrum from celebratory to condolence. Typically, the governor will preside over the opening of state-sponsored construction (highways, buildings) or of significant private investments. He or she will commemorate important historical dates, sign resolutions of state appreciation, and honor individuals or organizations for significant service. It is the governor who represents the condolences of the state in times of natural disasters or other times of trouble. In each of these cases the governor speaks for and represents all the state's citizens.

The governor also represents the state to external entities in an effort to promote the interests of the state. This role takes him to Washington, D.C., to governors' conferences and organizations of states (such as the National Association of States), and even to foreign lands. This latter is usually a reflection of the state's economic development efforts. Since modern federalism finds the federal government providing a large series of programs, regulations, and money, modern governors often find themselves expressing the state's views on federal actions and the competition for federal resources. In all these instances as chief of state, the governor largely transcends the political. Of course, though, you cannot completely separate the singular person from these two fundamental roles.

Chief of Government

The operational constitutional and extraconstitutional roles of the governor are clustered under the broad title of chief of government. They are distinguished from the chief of state roles by the fact that directly or indirectly they are instructed by political considerations. These are the roles the governor plays as a partisan politician.

Perhaps the most readily recognized of the roles in this category is that of *chief executive* (or *administrator*). This is a constitutionally defined role. Most of the administrative departments of government are impacted by the governor because he is responsible for seeing that the laws and programs of government are faithfully executed. Fourteen departments of government are defined in the constitution, have their head administrators or boards appointed by the governor, and report, at least in part, to the governor. In addition, there are hundreds of separate regulatory commissions, advisory boards, governing boards, and agencies with independent responsibilities, all of which have administrative heads or boards appointed by the governor as well. These give the governor the ability to reward supporters and gain allies, adding to his or her political clout. Another important opportunity for influencing public policy is given to the governor by his necessity to present an annual budget to the legislature in his role as chief executive.

This easily allows a transition to the second important role, that of *chief legislator.* This has both a constitutional and an extraconstitutional dimension. Constitutionally, the governor must provide an annual state-of-the-state address to the legislature, giving him yet another opportunity to influence priorities of public policy. More important, of course, is the power of the governor to veto legislation. This thrusts the governor into the entire legislative process not only because he can use his veto at the end of the process, but also because of the power he has simply in threatening the use of the veto. Legislators do not want to spend large amounts of time on bills if they know the governor will just veto them in the end. In addition, the governor's veto power is magnified by his powerful line-item veto on the budget. He can eliminate a line item or even lower the amount on any line. Responsibility for maintaining the balanced budget gives the governor the power to withhold spending if revenues fall short as well. The governor lobbies for those bills he supports throughout the process and can use legislative hearings to send members of the executive to testify in favor or against bills. The more purely political roles of the governor that are described below augment the ability of the governor to be effective with legislation as well.

There are a couple of constitutional roles that are narrower, but still the exclusive prerogative of the governor. First, the governor is the *military chief* for Missouri. The constitution gives him sole responsibility as commander in chief of the state national guard. This reserve, though paid for by the federal government and it can be called up to national service when needed, is used by the governor largely in times of natural disaster or, rarely, to deal with civil disturbances. A recent governor even loaned the guard for a short stint on the Mexican border to help Arizona deal with illegal immigration.

The other strict constitutional role is that of *ultimate judge*. In this role, the last appeal within the judicial system, the governor has the right to pardon (except for treason and impeachment), commute sentences, grant reprieves, and postpone the execution of sentences. Governors use this power sparingly, because there is great danger of a political backlash since someone given a commuted sentence, for example, could commit further crimes to the political detriment of the governor. Governor Carnahan, for example, acquiesced to a plea from the visiting pope in 1990 to commute a death sentence and found it to be a negative political issue in his next campaign (for the U.S. Senate). The governor does not have the right to grant paroles, a right given to some other governors. Being the ultimate judge includes the power of rendition, which is the ability to return a fugitive from justice to a state asking for the fugitive's return.

Two strictly political and extraconstitutional roles the governor enjoys are those of *head of the state party* and *leader of public opinion*. By virtue of being the highest state officeholder, the governor becomes the most prominent person with his party's label. The success or failure of a governor's administration echoes through his party's image, and thus the party tries hard to support its governor. This is true of the grassroots party up to and including the party in the legislature. The governor is not elected to any party office, nor is there a formal office as "head of the party" that the governor occupies. Still, it is clear that people perceive the governor as the chief spokesperson and representative of his or her political party. This is particularly true in a two-party, competitive state like Missouri, where party factions need to subsume their differences in favor of public unity in order to remain competitive in the next election. The governor does not have the power to control local nominations for public office, nor can he dictate party policy. Nevertheless, by careful use of his appointment powers and campaign assistance, the governor can guide support from party and legislators for his or her agenda.

The governor becomes leader of public opinion not simply because he has the title, but because the media focus on that role as the most recognized and responded to politician in state government. Wherever the governor goes, he gets at least local media attention and exposure. Even his role as chief of state exposes the governor, and almost always in a positive way. When he prioritizes particular issues through his repeated exposure, he inevitably raises those issues, those priorities, in the public dialogue. The governor has the best platform from which to try to mold public policy in the state. This does not mean the governor always benefits from being out front and the focus of media attention. This can also make him the target of any disgruntlement with government, regardless of whether the problem is within the governor's responsibility or ability to affect. Public exposure can work both ways, as we see daily in the media, whether with politicians or other public figures.

Separately, each of the roles that the governor plays gives the person in that role the ability to be an effective administrator and politician. The governor does share the statewide administrative responsibilities with the other state executives, but the rest have only limited abilities to affect public policy.

The Other Statewide Elected Executives

The *lieutenant governor* is primarily a spare tire, but being elected separately provides the office with the possibility of being a stepping-stone to other statewide office. Fundamentally, the job is to be available if something untoward happens to the governor and to preside over the Senate as ex-officio president of the Senate.

If the governor dies, is disabled, or is removed from office by impeachment and conviction, the lieutenant governor becomes the new governor and completes his term. As you might imagine, this rarely happens in any state and has never happened in Missouri. In former times if the governor were to leave the state, the lieutenant governor became the acting governor. Due to advanced technology in communications and transportation, this rarely has any substantive effect, since the governor is instantly available and can return in an emergency in short order. As ex-officio president of the Senate the lieutenant governor presides over the Senate and can vote in cases of ties. Beyond that, the role is pretty neutral. Since the role does not allow for participating in the debates or voting regularly on bills, lieutenant governors seldom preside over the deliberations of the Senate.

Because the job is so truncated, state law, including a referendum, has attempted to find things for the lieutenant governor to do. He or she serves as a member and secretary of the Board of Public Buildings and is the state volunteer coordinator and state ombudsman for the elderly; he is a member of the Board of Fund Commissioners and on the economic development, tourism, export boards and the housing development commission. All of these roles can make some impact if the governor gives resources and public exposure to the office. He is also an adviser to several offices in the Department of Education. All of which is to say that the lieutenant governor gets to go to a lot of meetings.

The *secretary of state* has three distinct areas of responsibility. First, the secretary is the custodian of the official acts, records, and documents dealing with the activities of the governor and the legislature. This includes being custodian of the state seal. All records need to have one official copy—that is the one submitted to the secretary of state who affixes the state seal. Virtually all states have this "secretarial" role.

The second area of responsibilities covers a variety of areas under state commerce. The secretary of state administers the Missouri Uniform Commercial Code, which deals with laws that regulate the registration, organization, and management of corporations in the state. Third, the secretary is the chief elections officer of the state. He or she must make sure that the placement of candidates for office, administration of elections, printing of ballots, and certification of the results are all done in concurrence with state law. Election-day problems in such states as Florida, Illinois, and Ohio demonstrate the importance of this seemingly straightforward administrative responsibility. In point of fact, of course, most of the election process is administered by the county clerks and election commissions in the Kansas

City and St. Louis areas. Since local candidates must be taken into consideration, ballots are printed by the local authorities, and these authorities set the physical polling places, get official judges, and count ballots (responsible for mechanisms that do so) for each polling station. They then report to the secretary of state, who certifies the results—particularly for statewide offices. These responsibilities rarely give the secretary input into public policy decision making, though having your name on so many things can give exposure. Secretaries have risen to higher office.

The *state treasurer* is essentially the state banker. The treasurer is the custodian of all state funds and distributes them as the General Assembly directs. All income of the state, whether from state or federal sources, is deposited with the treasurer's office. The treasurer then determines the short-term needs of the state and invests the rest of the funds either in interest-bearing bank accounts or in short-term government bonds. The placement must be approved by the governor and state auditor, though lately it is done by bids. Part of the state budget depends on the interest from such investments. Note that the treasurer also has little public policy decision-making role. This has often made it difficult politically to get the kind of public exposure necessary to set a foundation to run for governor or U.S. senator.

The *attorney general* (AG) is fundamentally the attorney for the state. Yet this simple description rebounds within a sweep of legal responsibilities reflected in the five divisions into which the attorney general's office is divided: litigation, criminal, trade offenses, government affairs, and human and environmental resources. All this and, of all things, this office is not constitutional but established by statute. Because local prosecutors do not have the resources to deal with appeals in cases in which the state is a party (suits and criminal cases), the attorney general's office prosecutes or defends at the appeals court and supreme court levels. The AG may institute suits to protect the state's interests, claims, or rights as well.

The AG represents the state in any challenge to the constitutionality of acts of the legislature or executive. The office is responsible for advising all elements of government when there is any question related to their duties. The formal interpretations of law and the constitution given by the AG do not have the power of law, however. It is in the areas of trade offenses and human and environmental resources in which the AG can make a great deal of political points for their personal political ambitions. These areas get the AG into protecting consumers and substantive policy areas such as the environment. Rogue companies (roofers, insurance frauds) or telemarketers who prey on the elderly and others are ripe areas for the AG to step in with legal action. Attorney generals find ample opportunities to get public exposure of their actions in protection of the state or its citizens. Several recent governors and U.S. senators have been attorneys general.

Another statewide elected official who is placed in a position to gain headlines and exposure to the public in a positive light is the *state auditor*. Although this office may not sound too exciting, the role of "watchdog" places the auditor in a position to constantly look like the protector of the citizens' money and as an exposer of corruption. The auditor's responsibility is to do two basic things: establish viable systems of accounting for state governments and audit the books of state governments. This means the auditor not only performs postaudit reviews (evaluating the audits of government agencies) but also critiques the methods of keeping financial records. It is not hard for the auditor to find something to correct in almost every review of the financial records of an agency. And these, of course, are the things the media pick up on. State auditors are often found on the ballot for governor or U.S. Senate; indeed, both Missouri senators in 2008 have held the position of state auditor.

The state auditor, then, audits every state agency, board, and commission. The office also deals with regular audits of third- and fourth-class counties and can be called upon to investigate the finances of any local government when petitioned by citizens. Because it handles all the state government's moneys, the constitution says the auditor must audit the treasurer's office every year.

It should be noted that all of the statewide officeholders are elected for four-year terms and except for the state auditor are elected in presidential election years. Because of the watchdog role of the auditor, this office is separated from the others on the statewide executive elections by being elected in the off-year cycle. Thus it is that the state auditor can often be in a position to run for governor or senator in the middle of the term without having to step down from his or her position.

Executive Bureaucracy

The bulk of Article IV deals not with the politically recognizable elected officials but with the operational bureaucratic administration. The heads of the departments are all appointed by the governor with the approval of the Senate. Care should be taken with this point, however, since some of the departments—that of education in particular—have boards that "head" the departments. These boards then choose a chief administrator who runs the day-to-day operation of the department.

Constitutional descriptions of the organization and purpose of the various departments vary from curt to more extensive. The Revenue Department description, for example, contains not only the basic role of collecting all taxes and fees but also adds other elements of state finances. It fixes the fiscal year from July 1 for twelve months. The governor's budgetary responsibilities are defined here as well: submission of budget, the line-item veto, and the ability to control the rate of spending to ensure balanced budget spending. The section also sets up a cash reserve fund, a facilities maintenance and review fund for the state, and rules for the withdrawal of moneys from the treasury. These are the kind of specifics most state constitutions leave to statutory law.

Because it has a large, independent source of income, the Transportation Department's organization and operation are extensively discussed in the constitution. With fewer specifics, but for the same reasoning of an independent taxing income, the Conservation and Natural Resources Departments also are explained with some specifics. The rest of the Article IV departments are simply established with short paragraphs. Two additional departments are allowed by the constitution to be established by the legislature. Thus, there can be sixteen departments in total. Missing from Article IV is the basic Elementary and Secondary Education Department. This important unit is part of and defined in Article IX, which deals with education.

Article IV:
The Executive Department in the Constitution

Article IV is entitled "Executive Department," but in reality it deals with many rather diverse segments of administration. The overall purpose is to carry into effect public policy that has been enacted into law and to perform other duties prescribed by the constitution and statutes. The article defines two types of executive officials: (1) elective—these include the governor, lieutenant governor, secretary of state, auditor, treasurer, and attorney general (except for the attorney general, interestingly enough, the qualifications and duties of these officials are outlined mostly by Sections 1–15); and (2) appointive—these officials (members of boards or commissions or administrative department heads) are appointed by the governor with the approval of the Senate.

Most of the departments are recognized in the constitution with a basic description, although some of their organization and many of their functions are described by statute. In most cases there are no sharp distinctions between the activities of departments headed by elected officials and those headed by appointed officials. The activities carried on by all departments are referred to broadly as "state administration." Nevertheless, how the constitution organizes the departments and the amount of independence each has been given are important and play a key role in the influence of that department.[1] Pay close attention, then, to whether the department is headed by an elected official—thus is more independent—or one appointed by the governor. Then note that some departments of the executive, though nominally in the governor's cabinet, have directive boards with a great deal of independence (such as the Transportation and Education Departments).

Sections 1–9 (and Others Pertaining to): The Governor

The constitution states in Article IV, Section 1, that the supreme executive power shall be vested in the governor. The duties of the governor are to take care that the laws are distributed and faithfully executed, and he is the conservator of the peace throughout the state (Section 2). Although the governor is charged with the duty of seeing that the laws are faithfully executed, the governor enjoys little authority derived from the mere fact that he is the chief executive of the state. His position in relation to the state administration is distinctly inferior to that of the president in relation to the national administration. The national constitution broadly bestows "the executive power" of the United States upon the president. There is no corresponding clause in the Missouri Constitution that concentrates executive power in the hands of the governor. On the contrary, the executive authority, as has been noted, is shared with other elected executive officials. The vague clause "conservator of the peace throughout the state" has not been a source of power for the governor in terms of the regular functions of his office, though his position as head of the National Guard could come into play here.

The Missouri Constitution outlines the qualifications for governor (Section 3): the governor shall be at least thirty years old and have been a citizen of the United States for at least fifteen years and a resident of Missouri at least ten years before election. These qualifications usually do not provoke much conflict, but in 1972 there was a question as to whether the Republican candidate for governor, Christopher Bond, satisfied the residency requirement. The Supreme Court of Missouri interpreted the word resident not to mean or require actual physical presence continuous and uninterrupted for ten years. A residence is a place where a man has his true fixed and permanent home and principal establishment and to which, whenever he is absent, he has the intention to return.[2] Mr. Bond had been out of the state to attend law school, clerk for a federal judge, and practice law. Another qualification placed on the governorship is that governors are limited to just two four-year terms. If a governor has for some reason served more than two years of a term, he can be elected only once (Section 17).

An important power of the governor, recognized in Section 4, is the power of appointment for all vacancies in public offices unless otherwise provided by law. Section 5 provides that the governor shall commission all officers unless another method of selection is provided by law. The governor makes appointments to boards and commissions and also appoints individuals to departments where a single director is provided. In filling these administrative offices, the governor seldom has a free hand. Members of administrative boards and commissions, and all department and division heads must be confirmed by the state's Senate (Section 51). Sometimes there are specific requirements for the positions (many boards must have an equal number Democrats and Republicans, for example), and for members of boards and commissions there are frequently constitutional or statutory restrictions fixing the definite and overlapping terms of their office. This often makes it impossible for the governor to appoint a majority of the members of a board or commission during a single term of office. All of these provisions, plus the fact that Missouri is gradually moving toward greater reliance on merit appointments for many departments, have tended to weaken the executive power of the governor.

Section 19 provides that all employees in the state welfare and penal institutions, and other state employees that the General Assembly shall determine, shall be selected on the basis of merit. Included in this section is a provision providing that any honorably discharged veteran would be given preference in examination and appointment as determined by law. Statutes make most department employees hired on a merit basis.

Article IV, Section 17, provides that the governor may remove all appointive officers, but because of the numerous restrictions on his appointive powers described above, his power of removal is limited.

The governor is given the authority of commander in chief (Section 6), which places him in command of the militia, and he may call out the militia to execute the laws, suppress actual and prevent threatened insurrection, and repel invasion. The governor also has the power to grant reprieves, commutations, and pardons to individuals convicted for all offenses except treason and crimes resulting in impeachment (Section 7).

These are traditional powers of chief executives and play only a limited and at best temporary role in the governor's ability to influence state government.

On the positive side of authority for the governor, there are several powers that give the governor substantial influence. He may give the General Assembly information as to the state of government and recommend for its consideration such measures as he deems necessary, and he may call the General Assembly into special session (Section 9). This latter event happened as recently as July 2010. As discussed earlier, these responsibilities, when used wisely, may allow the governor to become an influence of prime importance in shaping targeted legislation. By calling a special session and specifying the topics to be considered, the governor forces the legislature to consider only particular legislative matters.

Another major power that the governor has is his veto. Even every resolution that passes the General Assembly, except resolutions dealing with questions of adjournment, going into joint session, and amending the Missouri Constitution, must be signed by the governor in the same manner as a bill (Section 8). Thus, in effect, the governor has veto power over nearly all substantive actions of the General Assembly.

The governor also has major power in terms of the spending activities of the state. The governor is required to submit a budget for the next appropriation period, which must contain the estimated available revenues of the state and a complete and itemized plan of expenditures of the state within thirty days of the convening of the General Assembly in regular session. He must also provide recommendations for providing revenues sufficient to meet expenditures (Section 24). This allows the governor to provide an overall plan in terms of the financial activity of the state. Even though the General Assembly may change any part of the governor's budget, the general spending and revenue patterns in the state are influenced greatly by this budget.

In addition to the traditional veto of legislative action (Article III, Section 31), the governor has what is commonly referred to as the "item veto." Section 27 of Article IV describes the veto as allowing the governor to "object to one or more items or portions of items of appropriation of money in any bill presented to him, while approving other portions of the bill." He may not, however, reduce any appropriation for free public schools or for the payment of principal and interest on the public debt. There has been some controversy over whether the item veto applies to nonappropriation items in the budget. In 1973 the Supreme Court of Missouri ruled that only appropriation items were subject to the item veto.

Words that set out the purpose of the appropriation may not be stricken unless the money appropriated is vetoed.[3]

Another important power of the governor is the power to control the rate of spending in the state (Section 27). The governor may control the rate at which any appropriation by allotment or other means is spent and may reduce the expenditures of the state or any of its agencies below their appropriations whenever the actual revenues are less than the revenue estimates upon which the appropriations were based. This happened frequently in the low-income years of the early part of the twenty-first century. Higher education especially had its appropriations reduced by the governor to maintain a spending balance.

In summary, the power of the governor in terms of state expenditures is immense, and although he cannot appropriate, he is in the position to have a major impact on the funding of programs in the state. This power, of course, also enhances his power as chief executive since all state agencies are aware of his budgetary powers. In comparison with many other governors, the influence of the Missouri governor in this area is quite substantial.[4]

Sections 10–11: The Lieutenant Governor

The lieutenant governor, who must have the same qualifications as the governor, runs independently in Missouri. The lieutenant governor's functions are as follows: to succeed the governor in the event of the latter's death, removal, absence, disability, or impeachment and to preside over the deliberations of the Senate and to vote in case of a tie. He may also debate all questions in the committee of the whole. There was some controversy over the role that the lieutenant governor was to play in the Senate, and the Supreme Court of Missouri ruled that the Senate itself had the power to delegate such duties as who shall assign bills to committees and who shall rule on points of order. As noted in the legislative chapter, the Senate gives these responsibilities (powers) to the president pro tem of the Senate.[5] Thus, the lieutenant governor has the right to preside over the deliberations, but any power he might exercise in that capacity is determined by the Senate, and, at the present time, the Senate has not turned over any procedural power. The lieutenant governor serves on a number of boards as outlined above, but there is little power that results from these activities.

Article IV also provides for the order of succession to the governorship (Section 11[a]). The line of succession is lieutenant governor, president pro tempore of the Senate, Speaker of the House, secretary of state, state auditor, and attorney general. A disability board is provided, which is composed of the lieutenant governor, the secretary of state, the state auditor, the state treasurer, the attorney general, president pro tempore of the Senate, the Speaker of the House, the majority floor leader of the Senate, and the majority floor leader of the House (Section 11[b]). Whenever a majority of this board transmits to the president pro tempore and the Speaker of the house a written declaration that the governor is unable to discharge the powers and duties of his office, whoever is next in line will immediately assume the powers and duties of the office as acting governor. In case of a dispute as to a governor's ability to carry out the office, the state supreme court would decide. If any state officer other than the lieutenant governor were to act as governor, the duties of his regular office would be performed by their chief administrative assistant (Section 11[c]).

Section 11 provides for a number of contingencies and usually is not a source of conflict. Nevertheless, in 1991 there developed a major dispute over the interpretation of Section 11(a). The specific phrase was "absence from the state." The question was under what conditions could the lieutenant governor assume certain powers of the governor when the governor was absent from the state. The constitutional provision that gave rise to this practice states, "On the failure to qualify, absence from the state or other disability of the governor, the powers, duties and emoluments of the governor shall devolve upon the lieutenant governor for the remainder of the term or until the disability is removed." Historically, this provision was followed by governors whenever they left the state. This procedure was challenged by Governor John Ashcroft in regard to his absence from the state February 12, 1990, to February 27, 1990, since he faxed his signature for official business and thought this legal. The secretary of state refused to authenticate the signatures. As a result of this action by the secretary, the governor sought a court order (a "writ of mandamus"), directing the secretary of state to accept, authenticate, and attest the documents.[6]

The Supreme Court of Missouri in its decision noted that there were a number of jurisdictions with provisions that were essentially the same as Article IV, Section 11(a), of the Missouri Constitution and that these provisions had been interpreted to mean that the power of governor would devolve to the lieutenant governor when the governor would leave the state. This was described as the "physical absence" rule. The court noted that other jurisdictions had adopted the "effective absence" principle, which held that the power of the governor would devolve to the lieutenant governor only when such absence effectively prevented the governor from executing the duties of his office. The court argued that this "effective absence" approach was a precedent in Missouri, since it had been used in 1883 when the court had stated, "The absence of the governor from the state, for the purpose of performing a duty cast upon him by law, did not authorize the lieutenant-governor to assume the functions of his office during such absence and receive his salary."[7]

Thus, the only question to decide was whether the governor could function in terms of the activities at issue when he was out of the state. The court ordered the secretary of state to accept the governor's actions, since the governor's execution of the various functions at issue in the case were made possible by his facsimile signature pursuant to instructions communicated by "fax" and by telephone. Thus, the Supreme Court of Missouri had changed constitutional interpretation to suit modern technological changes.

Section 12: Executive Department

This section states that all elective and appointed employees except for those in the legislative and judicial branches are part of the executive. It articulates the six elected statewide officials and then limits the number of departments to fifteen plus the office of administration. There are thirteen specific departments cited by the constitution plus the Office of Administration (the Departments of Agriculture, Conservation, Economic Development, Natural Resources, Elementary and Secondary Education [defined in Article IX], Higher Education, Highways and Transportation, Labor and Industrial Relations, Public Safety, Revenue, Insurance, Mental Health, and Social Services). In addition, the constitution allows for the formation of up to two others by the legislature (currently the Department of Corrections and the Department of Health). This brings the total to fifteen departments plus the Office of Administration. The constitution then lists the elective officials and their responsibilities (besides governor and lieutenant governor, which are already covered) followed by the administrative departments.

Section 13: State Auditor

The state auditor's office is the state's independent "watchdog" agency. Candidates for state auditor must meet the same qualifications as those for governor. The basic functions of the office are detailed by statute.[8] The auditor is charged with providing an appropriate system of accounting for all public officials of the state, and with conducting annual postaudits of the accounts of all state agencies and an audit of the state treasury. The auditor makes all other audits and all investigations required by law and gives an annual report to the governor and the General Assembly. The office also establishes appropriate systems of accounting for the political subdivisions of the state, supervises their budgeting systems, and audits their accounts as provided by law (Section 13). This office can be a very important one in terms of pointing out various activities where departments are not carrying out their functions. In addition, it can become involved with local subdivisions when it is called in by citizen petition to do an audit. Beyond the formal qualifications for the office, in recent years there has been a political emphasis on having a certified public accountant occupy the office. Whereas all the other statewide elected officials are elected in presidential election cycles, the auditor is elected in the off years (Section 17).

Section 14: Secretary of State

The secretary of state is the custodian of the seal of the state and authenticates all official acts of the governor except the approval of laws (Section 14). The specific functions of the office are described by statute.[9] The office is also responsible for collecting, compiling, sorting, and publishing a variety of state documents. The office acts as the state's election officer. It handles declarations of candidates for office where the election involves more than one county; county clerks or local election commissions do the rest. Election results and campaign financial reports are also collected and certified by the secretary. In addition, the secretary of state oversees several areas in regard to state commerce—for example, administration of the Missouri Uniform Commercial Code and registration of corporations and securities.

Section 15: State Treasurer

The duties of the state treasurer, as defined by Section 15, are to be custodian of all state funds, determine the amount of state moneys not needed for current operating expenses, and invest such moneys not needed for current operations in time deposits bearing interest. These must be placed either in Missouri banking institutions selected by the state treasurer and approved by the governor and state auditor or in short-term U.S. government bonds. The operation of the office is essentially a banking function.[10]

The state treasurer is a member of the State Board of Fund Commissioners, the Missouri Housing Development Commission, and the board of trustees of the Missouri State Employees' Retirement System. Holders of this office are limited, like the governor, to two four-year terms (Section 17).

Note on the Attorney General

It is quite interesting that the duties of the attorney general's office are not detailed in the constitution, for the office is an important one. Instead, the duties are outlined by statute.[11] The attorney general is probably second only to the governor in terms of importance as a state official. The attorney general represents the legal interests of Missouri, and of its people as a group, but he cannot represent individual citizens in private legal actions. As the state's chief legal officer, the attorney general must prosecute or defend all appeals to which the state is a party, including every felony criminal case that is appealed to the Supreme Court of Missouri and courts of appeals. He is also required to institute, in the name and on behalf of the state, all civil suits and other proceedings that are necessary to protect the state's rights, interests, or claims. He also may appear, interplead, answer, or defend any proceedings in which the state's interests are involved.

The attorney general renders official opinions to the General Assembly, the governor, the secretary of state, the auditor, the treasurer, the heads of the various departments, and the circuit or prosecuting attorneys on questions of law relating to their duties. These opinions, however, have no force of law, and the Supreme Court of Missouri has ruled that they have no more weight than the opinion of any competent attorney.[12] Despite this, they are still frequently sought and do have some impact on state policy. In addition, the attorney general may institute proceedings to determine by what authority any corporation is doing business in the state and if there have been any violations of its franchise or of state laws.[13] He may also assist in the proceedings against any person not subject to impeachment, that is, elected or appointed to any county, city, town, or township office who is unlawfully holding office, or may move to oust any public official for misfeasance, nonfeasance, or malfeasance in office.[14]

Sections 17–21: Executive Department Miscellaneous

These sections set term limits on the governor and treasurer and the election cycle for all but the auditor during presidential election cycles.

Section 17 also says the governor shall appoint all heads of the executive departments. Election returns are verified by the secretary of state with help from a board of state canvassers made up of disinterested judges. Interestingly, any tie vote is decided by the General Assembly.

These sections set a merit system for the executive department, place their headquarters in Jefferson City, and disallow any raise during the terms of office of the elected officials.

Sections 22–28: Department of Revenue

The Department of Revenue is authorized by Section 22 of Article IV. The primary duties of the department are the collection of taxes, titling and registration of motor vehicles, and licensing of drivers.[15] The director is appointed by the governor and confirmed by the Senate. Five divisions administer the operations of the department: Division of Administration, Division of Information Systems, Division of Motor Vehicles and Drivers Licensing, Division of Taxation and Collection, and Division of Compliance. The Highway Reciprocity Commission, State Tax Commission, Horse Racing Commission, and State Lottery Commission are organized within the department, but because of their sensitivity they are administered separately.

Sections 29–34: Highways and Transportation Department

The State Highway and Transportation Department is a huge department that is governed by a bipartisan State Highway and Transportation Commission, composed of six members appointed by the governor with the consent of the Senate (Section 29). The members of the commission are appointed to staggered terms of six years each. No more than three commissioners may be members of the same political party. The chief engineer, who is the chief operating officer of the department, is appointed by the commission. This organizational structure provides some autonomy from influence by the governor, as a new governor would have to deal with commissioners appointed by his predecessor and would need two terms to appoint a majority. Even then the commission makes decisions on its own. The Highway and Transportation Commission has authority over all state transportation programs and facilities, including bridges, highways, aviation, railroads, mass transportation, ports, and waterborne commerce and has the authority to limit access to, from, and across state highways when the public interest requires it. Another source of autonomy for the department is a result of the sources of funds for the department. Most of its revenue comes from earmarked funds such as motor vehicle fuel taxes, licenses and fees, and part of one-half of the motor vehicle sales tax. In addition, federal gas tax funds are an important source of revenue.

The funds available to the department that are not the result of legislative appropriations must be used for purposes outlined in Sections 30(a)–34. Section 30(a) provides the department direction as to the apportionment of the motor vehicle fuel tax. In detail it provides for the percentage going to a special trust fund known as the County Aid Road Trust Fund and provides a basis to allocate money from this fund to the counties. Also, funds are provided for cities, towns, and villages for specific purposes, and a basis is provided for the allocation of these funds.

Section 30(b) provides a list of the order of the use of funds in terms of priorities and the authorized projects for which funds may be expended. For example, payment of principal and interest on any outstanding state roads bonds must be paid before any other use of the funds can be made. An interesting question developed over the interpretation of this section when the spending of money by the department for signs indicating food, fuel, and lodging was questioned as to whether this constituted an improvement to highways. The Supreme Court of Missouri ruled that these signs did constitute an improvement to the highway system.[16]

The authority of the highway and transportation commission is defined further in Sections 30(c)–32. These sections are much like statutory law in that they detail the powers of an administrative agency.

Sections 33 and 34 are basically housekeeping provisions that protect an employee's retirement rights in case of transfer (Section 33) and accept the outstanding bonds issued under another constitutional provision as legitimate obligations of the state (Section 34).

Sections 35–36: Department of Agriculture

This department functions under the supervision of the director of agriculture, who is appointed by the governor with the consent of the Senate (Section 35). The department is charged with enforcing state laws regulating the handling and marketing of agricultural products and exists to protect producers, processors, distributors, and consumers of food and fiber and to promote and serve Missouri's agricultural industry.[17] Included under the agriculture provisions is Section 36, which allows the General Assembly to enact laws to encourage forestry and prevent and suppress forest fires on private lands.

Section 36(a): Department of Economic Development

The Department of Economic Development is under the supervision of a director appointed by the governor with the consent of the Senate. The department is to administer all programs provided by law relating to the promotion of the economy of the state, the economic development of the state, trade and business, and other activities and programs affecting the economy of the state (Section 36[a]).[18]

Section 36(b): Department of Insurance

Added in 1990, this department's role is to be defined by the legislature, although the section mandates an office of consumer affairs to investigate unlawful acts in connection with the department's responsibilities.

Section 37: Department of Social Services

The Department of Social Services is charged with protecting the health and general welfare of the people (Section 37). The director is appointed by the governor with the consent of the Senate. It is an "umbrella agency" that coordinates and integrates many programs.[19] Probably the key responsibility is the administration of programs that provide public assistance to the elderly and specialized assistance to young people in conflict with or in flight from their home environments. The director has the major responsibility of administering federal, state, and local funds with the efficiency required to produce the best possible use of available resources.

Sections 37(a)–39: Department of Mental Health

The Department of Mental Health is administered by a director who is appointed by a seven-member commission with the consent of the Senate. The commissioners are appointed to four-year terms by the governor with confirmation by the Senate. The department is to provide treatment, care, education, and training for persons suffering from mental illness or retardation and has administrative control of the state hospitals and other institutions and centers established for these purposes (Section 37[a]).[20]

Sections 40(a)–46: Department of Conservation

The control, management, restoration, conservation, and regulation of the bird, fish, game, forestry, and all wildlife resources of the state, including hatcheries, sanctuaries, refuges, reservation, and all other property owned, acquired, or used for such purposes, are vested in the Conservation Commission by Section 40(a).[21] The commission consists of four members appointed by the governor with the consent of the Senate, not more than two of whom shall be of the same party. Members serve six-year staggered terms. The commission appoints the director of conservation, who in turn appoints assistants and other employees deemed necessary by the commission. The commission determines salaries and qualifications of the director and all employees of the departments (Section 42).

The commission arrangement makes the department quite independent and powerful. In addition, Section 41 provides it with the power of eminent domain. Another important source of power is money from a one-eighth of 1 percent sales tax and a one-eighth of 1 percent use tax (Section 43[a] and [b]), which is earmarked for conservation purposes. There are some constitutional restrictions in terms of the operation of the Conservation Commission, but in comparison to the other departments of state government, it is quite unique in terms of its independence from the regular political processes and its independent source of income.

Sections 47(a)–47(c): Department of Natural Resources

The Department of Natural Resources administers the programs of the state as provided by law relating to environmental control and the conservation and management of natural resources (Section 47).[22] The director is appointed by the governor with the consent of the Senate. Section 47(a) provides sales and use taxes to be levied for soil and water conservation and for state parks. The use and sales taxes are levied at one-tenth of 1 percent. Revenue raised from these taxes is to be divided equally between the Soil and Water Sales Tax Fund and the Park Sales Tax Fund. These funds are to be expended by appropriations by the General Assembly for the saving of soil and water resources, for the conservation of the productive power of agricultural land, and for the acquisition, development, maintenance, and operation of state parks.

Section 48: Department of Public Safety

The Department of Public Safety is charged with the administration of programs provided by law to protect and safeguard the lives and property of the people of the state (Section 48). The director is appointed by the governor with the consent of the Senate. The major responsibility is the coordination of all elements of law enforcement, criminal investigation, and public safety activities undertaken by state government. Its major element is the state police force, which focuses on the highway system.[23] The latest addition to the responsibilities of an office within this department is to coordinate homeland security. This has added importance to the department, but despite its many responsibilities in coordinating law enforcement in the state, law enforcement still is primarily a function carried out by municipal and county governments.

Section 49: Department of Labor and Industrial Relations

The Labor and Industrial Relations Commission governs the operation of the Department of Labor and Industrial Relations, and is composed of three members (Section 49). Each commissioner is appointed by the governor with the consent of the Senate. The constitutional provisions dealing with qualifications of commission members are rather detailed. One member must be classified as a representative of employers, one member must be classified as a representative of employees, and one member must be classified as representing the public and must be licensed to practice law in the state of Missouri. No more than two members of the commission may be of the same political party. The governor appoints a chair from the commission members. The commission nominates and the governor appoints, with the consent of the Senate, a director of the department.

The department is responsible for administering programs that promote job placement, provide an income contribution for workers to offset the loss of job because of injury, provide an income contribution for workers to offset the loss of a job because of a layoff, resolve matters of majority representation and appropriate bargaining units, regulate wages for certain work in public works and construction, assist in the employment of the handicapped, and enforce Missouri's antidiscrimination statutes and protect Missouri citizens in the areas of housing, employment, and public accommodation.[24] In addition, the department administers the program of the state relating to the protection and improvement of human rights (Section 49). These are all important state administrative functions.

Section 50 and Others: Office of Administration

The Office of Administration is the state's service and administrative control agency.[25] The chief administrative officer is the commissioner. The office of administration has eight divisions: Accounting, Budget and Planning, Design and Construction, Data Processing and Telecommunications, Flight

Operations, General Services, Personnel, and Purchasing. The commissioner also directs statewide coordination of affirmative action and labor relations. The commissioner's role in the financial operations of the state is recognized by several other sections of Article IV. Section 27(a), which establishes a cash operating reserve fund, stipulates that the commissioner of administration has the power to make transfers from the cash operating reserve fund to general revenue or to transfer funds from general revenue to the cash fund. The conditions under which the transfers are to be made are spelled out in Section 27(a). The commissioner is also given a role by Section 28: it provides that no money may be withdrawn from the state treasury except by warrant drawn in accordance with an appropriation made by the General Assembly. The commissioner must certify such a warrant for payment and certify that the expenditure is within the purpose of the General Assembly appropriation and there is money to pay for the warrant. This is an important centralized clearinghouse function that allows the governor to keep track of the flow of moneys within state government.

Sections 51: Office of Administrator

A commissioner of administration helps the governor in administrating the executive department. The role is appointed by the governor with the advice and consent of the Senate. Section 51 says that all administrative heads are appointed in the same manner.

Section 52: Department of Higher Education

The Department of Higher Education is administered by the Coordinating Board of Higher Education, which consists of nine members appointed by the governor with the consent of the Senate. No more than five members shall be of the same political party (Section 52). The board is represented through each of Missouri's nine U.S. congressional districts, and the term of appointment is for six years. The board employs a commissioner to serve as its chief executive. The four major functions performed by the coordinating board are statewide planning for higher education and libraries, policy analysis, academic program approval and review for the public two-year and four-year colleges and universities, and budget recommendations to the governor and General Assembly for operating and capital financing for four-year colleges and universities. In 2007 the General Assembly, under constitutional guidelines, beefed up the role of coordination by the commission and gave the commissioner increased powers.[26]

Article IX, Section 2:
Department of Elementary and Secondary Education

This department was established in the education section of the constitution (Article IX). The State Board of Education is charged with the supervision of instruction in the public schools and consists of eight members appointed by the governor with the consent of the Senate for eight-year terms. No more than four of the members shall be from the same political party (Article IX, Section 2[a]). The terms are arranged so that only one term expires every year. The board appoints a commissioner of education, who serves as the chief administrative and executive officer of the Department of Elementary and Secondary Education (Article IX, Section 2[b]). The department is largely involved in assisting local school districts in carrying out the requirements prescribed by state law and in providing leadership in the improvement of the administration and instruction of the public schools of the state.[27]

The constitution allows two additional departments to be created by the General Assembly. As noted earlier, at the present time these two departments are the Department of Corrections and the Department of Health.[28]

Article IV, then, deals with the executive elements of state government, and as such it provides the administrative structure for the vast majority of individuals who work for the state of Missouri. The constitution strives for equality of access to these jobs in Section 53, which states, "The appointment of all members of administrative boards and commissions and of all departments and division heads and all the employees thereof shall be made without regard to race, creed, color, or national origin."

What is interesting about this structure is the diversity that exists within and between the various departments. The elected departments are, of course, independent from the governor but still dependent on the General Assembly for a budget and statutory direction. The departments with heads appointed by the governor are more dependent on the governor but must look to the General Assembly for budgetary and statutory direction. Several departments such as the Highway and Transportation Department (Section 29) and the Department of Conservation (Section 43) are quite independent of the governor, since they are under the commission format.

They are also somewhat independent of the legislature, since they have designated sources of revenue, gas tax for highways and a one-eighth of 1 percent tax for conservation, though it can be spent only for the purposes stated in the constitution.[29] The legislature still must appropriate the money, but because the funds are earmarked, these departments do not have to compete for revenue against all the other state agencies. Other departments, primarily the education ones, are governed under the commission format but are dependent upon the legislature for their revenue.

5

The Judiciary

In this chapter we are interested in describing the structure and functioning of the Missouri judicial system: Article V of the constitution. Because most laws, civil and criminal, are state laws, it follows that the greater load of the American judicial system falls upon the state court systems. The fundamentals of the American approach to justice apply to the state courts as well as to the federal courts, however, since they both operate under the same assumptions and judicial theory.

For example, the American judiciary operates on an *adversarial system.* That means that courts are fundamentally referees between two contestants. In civil cases the contestants are individuals challenging each other under the umbrella of civil laws. The courts, of course, are empowered to apply the law and thus are actually somewhat more than referees. The courts provide the structure for individuals (remember, in law, this means corporate as well as personal individuals) to solve conflicts, whether domestic disputes (divorce, child custody, and the like), property disputes (estate settlements), or economic contractual disputes or suits. In criminal cases the adversaries are, of course, the state, on the one hand, accusing an individual of criminal activity, on the other hand. Lawyers for both sides challenge each other on fact, motive, and points of law, while the courts make sure the game is played fairly and under the law.

Another foundation of our system is that the courts deal only with *justiciable disputes,* that is, disputes growing out of an actual case or controversy where someone has something real to lose: broadly, life, liberty, or property. American courts do not deal with hypothetical issues or give advisory opinions, as do some European court systems.

Perhaps the most important point to make is that state courts maintain the basic power of *judicial review* that is the mainstay of the judiciary's role in our system of checks and balances. The state courts of Missouri (ultimately the supreme court) may judge the constitutionality of the acts of the executive and the legislature of the state. This means that precedent (the use of previous court decisions to guide cases before the courts) is also a fundamental character of the Missouri system.

Judicial Structure

After introductions, this book has given a close rendering of the articles of the constitution. The close reading of Article V of the constitution that follows this introductory material can be confusing and make it hard to picture the structure of the Missouri judiciary if it is the only discussion of the structure. So a brief overview follows, giving hopefully a more coherent view of the whole system. Refer to Figure 5.1 for a graphic illustration as we discuss the judicial structure.

The federal court system is organized basically in three levels: the supreme court, the appeals courts, and the courts of original jurisdiction (trial courts). This is true of Missouri as well, but the fact that state courts deal with a plethora of civil and criminal statutes dealing with the day-to-day lives of its citizens creates the necessity for a more complex original jurisdiction level. Add to this the fact that most misdemeanor (minor) laws are state or local laws, and thus we understand the creation of a fourth court level to dispose of these cases—the lower level courts outlined in Figure 5.1. Within this complexity, Missouri has created what is called a "unified" court system that puts all the courts under one umbrella of coordination executed by the supreme court and a combined (specifically unified) administration at the third and fourth levels.

This is all in need of explanation. Since most of the work of the court system is done at the lower original, jurisdiction levels, we will discuss the top two levels briefly before attacking these levels. The *Supreme Court of Missouri* is fundamentally the last appeals level from the Missouri Court of Appeals and on rare occasions lower courts. It has exclusive jurisdiction over the validity of U.S. treaties or statutes contested within the state. The supreme court can evaluate any state statute and the constitution as well as revenue laws and titles to state office if challenged, and it must review all death sentences. It sets the final precedents under Missouri's law and constitution.

Figure 5.1.   *MISSOURI COURT SYSTEM*

SUPREME COURT

> 7 Judges
>> Exclusive jurisdiction: validity of U.S. treaty or statute, Missouri
>> statute or constitution review, revenue laws, death penalty cases
>> Jurisdiction over cases transferred from the court of appeals
> Nonpartisan Court Plan

COURT OF APPEALS

> Western District, 11 Judges   Kansas City
> Eastern District, 14 Judges   St. Louis City, St. Louis County
>   Cape Girardeau, Hannibal
> Southern District, 7 Judges   Springfield, Poplar Bluff
> Jurisdiction: All appeals not within supreme court exclusive
>   jurisdiction. Remedial writs.
> Nonpartisan Court Plan

CIRCUIT COURT

> 45 Circuits   Every county within one of the 45
>   134 Total Circuit Judges
>   175 Total Associate Circuit Judges
>   336 Total Municipal Judges
> Nonpartisan Court Plan--St. Louis City, St. Louis County,
>   Jackson, Platte, and Clay Counties
> Partisan Elections--Rest of the state

CIRCUIT COURT DIVISIONS

> **Circuit Divisions** ⟺ **Juvenile Divisions**
> Jurisdiction   Jurisdiction
> Civil cases over $25K   Juvenile cases
> Domestic relations
> Felonies and misdemeanors

Associate Divisions ⟹ **Probate Divisions**   **Municipal Divisions**

Jurisdiction   Jurisdiction   Jurisdiction
Civil actions under $25K   Guardianships   Municipal traffic violations
Small claims court   Conservatorships   Municipal ordinances
Misdemeanors and infractions   Descendant estates
Felonies prior to filing of   Mental health claims
   the information
May handle all circuit
   court cases on assignment

There are seven judges on the court who hear and decide cases collegially. They make decisions on a majority vote with the same options as those available to the federal judges—majority opinion, concurring opinions, and dissenting opinions. Except for the exclusive areas of jurisdiction and death sentences, the court is the judge of its own cases; that is, it takes only the cases appealed to it that it wishes to hear. Usually, the court takes cases that are of great public interest, are areas of interpretation either not taken before, or have conflicting decisions from lower courts.

The leader of the court is the chief justice. The constitution allows the justices to choose their own chief, which they do, giving each a two-year term in the position. This role is not only the "chair" of the court's meetings; it is also the chief administrative officer of the court system, taking care of day-to-day operations and overall direction of the entire court system. As "chair" the chief justice assigns cases to judges for the official rulings of the case and presides over all their meetings. The judges must be thirty years old and U.S. citizens for fifteen years as well as qualified Missouri voters for nine years. The judges are chosen for twelve-year terms by a nonpartisan court plan called a "merit plan" or, since Missouri was the first to adopt it, the "Missouri Plan." We'll explain this later.

The *court of appeals* takes appeals from courts of original jurisdiction. The specific number of justices and geographical range of responsibility of the court are given to the legislature to decide. Currently, the court is divided into three districts, each administered separately. They are the Western District, which has eleven judges; the Eastern District, with fourteen judges; and the Southern District, with seven judges. The differing number of judges reflects the caseload history of the districts. The courts generally deal with cases using three-judge panels. A majority vote of the three decides the cases. All the judges on the appeals courts have twelve-year terms and the same qualifications as supreme court justices. They are also appointed in the same manner—by the "Missouri Plan."

Statewide the *circuit court* level of the system contains the following: 45 numbered, separate circuits; 134 total circuit judges; 175 total associate circuit judges; and 336 municipal judges, all illustrated in Figure 5.1. Note this cumulative box summarizes the total of circuits. The lower box illustrates each circuit. Every county in the state is within one of the 45 circuits, which are organized around the county boundaries. Each circuit, though, is not equal in size, population, or number of counties within its jurisdiction. Since counties vary in size and population, the circuits are not equal, and there are varying numbers of judges in circuits. Large populated circuits have more judges, smaller ones fewer. For instance, most rural circuits have only one circuit division judge as well as one associate division judge for each county within its jurisdiction. Associate division judges are basically county judges, then. In larger counties there is more than one associate division judge. Caseload has dictated the number of circuit and associate circuit judges in each circuit.

When you look at the box covering the *circuit court division* of the system in Figure 5.1 (the lower box), you might get confused. The basic point to keep in mind is that there are fundamentally two levels to each circuit court: the circuit division and the associate division. The circuit division handles largely civil cases with more than twenty-five thousand dollars involved, domestic relations, and felony criminal cases as a court of original jurisdiction (the trial level where the court makes the first disposition on the case). This court may also deal with misdemeanors in some instances. The circuit court judge is also responsible for the juvenile justice system (including oversight of juvenile officers) within the circuit. If there is more than one judge at the circuit division level, the judges choose a chief judge who administers the division and assigns judges to cases. Sometimes there may be one of the judges assigned to specialize in the juvenile court. If there is but a singular judge for the division, they take care of this area as well as all the others. The judges at this level serve for six-year terms.

The *associate divisions* (county courts) deal with civil actions under twenty-five thousand dollars, misdemeanor infractions, small claims court, and traffic court outside of municipalities (if there is a municipal judge). Preliminary hearings of felonies are often handled by the associate division judges also, to allow the circuit-level judges to focus on their trial work. The associate division includes the probate division, as this level covers the probate areas of responsibility: guardianships, conservatorships, descendant estates, and mental health proceedings. This is the nitty-gritty level of the court system in that it deals with the day-to-day order and conflicts in the lives of people down where they live.

Each county must have at least one resident associate division judge— large counties may have several. Singular, largely rural, county judges must deal with the full range of cases assigned to their division. They divide their time among misdemeanors, traffic court, small claims court (where the aggrieved can file a complaint concerning less than fifteen hundred dollars inexpensively and without a lawyer), and probate court problems. Larger counties with several judges often share the responsibilities by specializing in one of the areas of the court's activities, though they need to be flexible and available where the caseload is at any particular time.

Municipalities (cities, towns) of any size tend to have their own municipal courts. Again, the large municipalities may have a number of judges. This court deals with misdemeanors that arise from municipal codes, ordinances, and regulations. Traffic violations within the municipality often dominate the docket. Most municipal judges are appointed by the municipal government.

The chief justice of the circuit division (chosen by the member judges of the circuit) is in charge of the operations of the whole circuit—both the circuit division and the associate division. This is the core of the "unified" judiciary at the original jurisdiction level and why they are symbolically illustrated in Figure 5.1 by being in a singular box. For example, associate judges can be, and are, assigned felony and serious civil trials at the higher level when they are needed due to either caseload or the absence of circuit division judges for one reason or another. The unification brings uniform administration and flexibility to the circuits.

Judges are chosen in Missouri by either the Nonpartisan (Merit) Plan or by direct election. The Nonpartisan Plan is often called the Missouri Plan, since it originated in this state and some version has been adopted by nineteen other states. The Missouri Plan works by combining appointment with voter approval. It has the following elements. First, a nonpartisan seven-person commission is created to recommend three judges to the governor for any vacancy at the supreme court or appeals court levels. One member is selected from among the supreme court judges, three are appointed by the state bar association, and three citizens are appointed by the governor. The governor chooses one from the commission's three recommendations, and that judge serves for a year and then is put before the voters for retention or not.

At the circuit court level only judges in the three large municipal areas are chosen on the Missouri Plan—those in St. Louis City, St. Louis County; the Kansas City area counties (Jackson, Clay, and Platte); and Green County (Springfield). All other judges at the circuit level are elected in partisan elections. They are on the ballot by party and must campaign for election. Nonurban populations believed that it was good to check the traditional corruption of the urban political machines but thought they know their local leaders well and wanted to be able to choose who should fill the important role of local judges. Details are outlined in the discussion of Section 25 below.

Governor Blunt in 2007 raised the issue of the viability of this process because the commissions meet in private to make their choices. Because he did not like the choices given to him for a supreme court vacancy, there was a public discussion of changing to a system of strict appointment by the governor. Even though one of his choices was a fellow Republican twice appointed to lower court positions, Blunt argued that the governor needed to be able to choose someone he believed did not "legislate" from the bench. Opposition pointed to the success of the Nonpartisan Plan. Others suspected that even the nonpartisan selection plan could be manipulated by partisan forces. This discussion continues not only in Missouri but in other states as well.

Article V:
The Judicial Department in the Constitution

The Missouri courts perform a number of very significant functions: (1) they provide means for the orderly adjustment of disputes between individuals and between individuals and state or local governments; (2) they constitute the instrumentality for determining the guilt or innocence of persons accused of violating the criminal laws of Missouri; (3) they, along with the federal courts, serve as guardians of the constitutional rights of the citizen against infringement by governmental authorities; and (4) they perform certain nonjudicial administrative duties such as the appointment of personnel and determining the rules of practice and procedure for all courts and administrative tribunals. As Justice William J. Brennan Jr., has noted, "The significance of the role of state courts in dispensing justice becomes greater each day. Without detracting in the slightest from the work of the federal courts, it is fair to say that the decisions that affect people's day-to-day lives most fundamentally are increasingly made by state courts."[1] After all, most laws—criminal and civil—are state laws; thus, they must be adjudicated within the state courts.

The Missouri constitutional provisions concerning the judiciary underwent significant revision in 1976 to the extent that nearly the entire judicial department (Article V) was revised. The purpose of the extensive revisions was to provide Missouri with what is called a "unified court system." State courts had for years been criticized for their extreme fragmentation, and Missouri's court system prior to the 1976 reforms fitted the pattern of fragmentation and inefficiency. The basic thrust of the reform was to centralize management, cooperation, and rule making.

In addition, the 1976 reforms meant that the state would assume more responsibility for the financial costs of the judicial system, relieving some of the burden from local governments.[2] One of the results of the reforms was the upgrading of salaries of state judges and court personnel. Another change that was promoted by the Missouri bar and included in the 1976 reform was the requirement that every supreme, appellate, circuit, and associate circuit court judge must be licensed to practice law in the state (Section 21). Prior to this, lower-court judges did not have to meet this requirement.

Sections 1–14: Supreme Court

The judicial power under the Missouri Constitution resides in a supreme court; a court of appeals, consisting of districts as prescribed by law; and circuit courts (Section 1). The Supreme Court is the highest court, and its jurisdiction is coextensive with the state boundaries. Its decisions are binding on all other courts. It is composed of seven judges and holds sessions in Jefferson City (Section 2).

The appellate jurisdiction of the supreme court is detailed in Section 3 and covers all cases involving the validity of treaty or statute of the United States or of a statute or provision of the constitution of Missouri, the construction of the revenue laws, the title to any state office, and in all cases where the punishment to be imposed is death.[3] If the case falls in one of these categories, it must be heard on appeal by the supreme court because it has exclusive appellate jurisdiction in such cases. Unless a case involves one of these questions, the party appealing the lower court's decision must take its appeal to the proper district of the court of appeals.

The power to declare an act of the legislature unconstitutional is a great power. This power to make a final determination of a question of law is a nondelegable power resting exclusively with the judiciary. The legislature may not preclude judicial review of judicial or quasi-judicial decision making by legislative or executive agencies.[4] Several decisions of the Supreme Court of Missouri have addressed the standards the court would use in assessing the validity of a statute. For example, the assumption will be that statutes are constitutional and will be found unconstitutional only if they clearly violate a constitutional provision—in other words, any doubt will be resolved in favor of the law's validity.[5] In order for a statute to be valid, it must give a person of ordinary intelligence a reasonable opportunity to learn what is prohibited. The statute must provide explicit standards against arbitrary and discriminatory application. In making a determination, the court will ascribe to the words the meaning that the people understand the words to have when the provision is adopted. The meaning conveyed is presumed to be the ordinary and usual meaning, which is derived from the dictionary.[6] The power of judicial review under the Missouri Constitution is much more constrained than under the national Constitution, since amendments to the state constitution are easily proposed and easily passed. Thus, decisions of the Missouri court can be checked by the public, which is not true of the national courts.

The constitutional limitation on the jurisdiction of the Supreme Court of Missouri means that most cases, which ordinarily involve routine questions of law, are appealed to the court of appeals, which generally has the last word. Cases pending in a court of appeals may be transferred to the supreme court when any participating judge dissents from the majority opinion and certifies that he deems the opinion of the court of appeals to be contrary to any previous decision of the supreme court or the court of appeals. Cases pending in the court of appeals may also be transferred to the supreme court by order of the majority of the judges of the participating district of the court, after opinion or by order of the supreme court, or before or after opinion by the court of appeals because of the general interest or importance of a question involved in the case, for the purpose of reexamining the existing law, or pursuant to supreme court rule—that is, request (Section 10).

Sections 7 and 9 also deal with transfers to the supreme court from divisions of the supreme court, but the procedure outlined is not used since the supreme court no longer sits in divisions. A party may seek transfer from the court of appeals, but the supreme court has discretion in terms of hearing the case. A case can be transferred to the supreme court when it is determined that a question of general interest or importance is involved or that the laws should be reexamined. A case conflicting with an earlier appellate court ruling can also be transferred. The Supreme Court of Missouri accepts cases in much the same manner as the U.S. Supreme Court, by transferring cases or accepting appeals that involve important and perhaps new or unusual issues. This allows the supreme court to select issues that it wishes to hear.

In addition, the supreme court establishes rules relating to practice, procedure, and pleading for all courts and administrative tribunals, which have the force and effect of law. These rules do not change substantive rights or the laws relating to evidence, the oral examination of witnesses, the right of trial by jury, or the right of appeal. Any of these rules may be annulled or amended in whole or in part by a statutory law limited to that purpose (Section 5).

The supreme court is authorized to establish rules of practice and procedure for all Missouri courts. These rules have the force of law, and if there is a conflict between the supreme court's rules and a statute, the rule always prevails if it addresses practice, procedure, or pleadings.[7] These rules cover all of the procedure necessary for the uniform handling of cases, such as times for filing motions and briefs, setting bail bonds, and the many other details with which the courts must deal. The court also prescribes the form and content of instructions that are read to juries in civil and criminal cases. In addition, all lawyers practicing law in Missouri must be licensed by the supreme court, which also disciplines lawyers for violations of the legal rules of professional conduct.[8]

The supreme court holds three sessions each year—beginning in January, May, and September—to hear oral arguments in cases on appeal. The judges of the supreme court then elect from their number a chief justice to preside over the court, usually for a two-year term. The chief justice of the supreme court is the chief administrative officer of the judicial system and, subject to the supervisory authority of the full court, supervises administration of the courts of Missouri (Section 8).

Section 4 allows the supreme court to appoint an office of state courts administrator, who is to aid the supreme court with the supervision of the lower courts. This office administers programs affecting all courts in the state, oversees the handling of federal aid funds awarded to the courts, and handles the transfer of judicial personnel between courts. The supreme court may make temporary transfers of judicial personnel from one court or district to another (Section 6). The office of state courts administrator also has responsibility for the classification and payroll of judicial personnel throughout the forty-five judicial circuits.

The judges on the supreme court have terms of twelve years. They are appointed through the Missouri nonpartisan court plan and may have successive terms. They must have been citizens of the United States for at least fifteen years and qualified voters of Missouri for nine years preceding their selection. They must be at least thirty years of age (Sections 19, 21, and 25[a]).

Each year the supreme court decides several hundred cases. Some of its most difficult cases, and those involving the most sensitive legal issues, are those concerning extraordinary remedies that can be sought directly from the supreme court without following the usual procedure through the lower courts. The most frequently sought remedies are prohibition (asking that a judge be stopped from issuing an order or proceeding in a case), mandamus (asking that a public official be directed to perform a certain task), ouster (seeking the removal from office of a public official), and habeas corpus (seeking the release of a person who is allegedly being held in the improper custody of the state). In addition, with the legalization of the death penalty in Missouri and the requirement that the court hear all cases dealing with the death penalty, the court is the focus of intense interest in many death penalty cases.

Section 12 requires that all opinions of the supreme court and courts of appeals be in writing and filed in the respective cases and that they become a part of the record of the court. These are currently published in *The South Western Reporter*.

The Supreme Court of Missouri plays a very important role in the operation of the state political system. Many of the most controversial issues of state government are resolved at this level. An example of this was a case where two amendments on the ballot at the same election were in conflict. The court solved the potential confusion by ruling that both could stay on the ballot and the amendment with the largest number of affirmative votes would be controlling.[9]

Section 13: Court of Appeals

The court of appeals has general appellate jurisdiction in all cases except those within the exclusive jurisdiction of the Supreme Court (Section 3). Section 13 provides that the court shall be organized into separate districts, the number—not less than three—of geographical boundaries and territorial jurisdiction to be determined by the General Assembly. The General Assembly has authorized three districts: an Eastern District headquartered in St. Louis, a Southern District headquartered in Springfield, and a Western District headquartered in Kansas City. The courts may meet in different locations, though.

The number of judges for each district is also determined by the General Assembly. Judges on the court of appeals are to have the same qualifications as judges for the supreme court and are appointed for twelve years. Each district of the court of appeals has general supervisory control over courts and tribunals in its jurisdiction. The judges in the court operate usually as three-judge panels. Each district of the court of appeals elects from its number a chief judge who then serves as the chief administrative officer of the district. The term of service is determined by the courts over which they preside, but two years is typical.

Sections 14–23: Circuit Courts

The circuit courts have original jurisdiction in all cases and matters, civil and criminal (Section 14). The state is divided into forty-five convenient circuits of contiguous counties, and each circuit has at least one circuit judge. The number of judges and the geographical boundaries of a circuit are determined by the General Assembly. Each circuit has a presiding judge, who is chosen by secret ballot of the circuit and associate circuit judges of each circuit and has general administrative authority over the court (Section 15).

A circuit court may be separated into divisions, and the circuit judges in each are assigned to the various divisions by the presiding judge. For example, in Jackson County's circuit level, judges are assigned to various divisions such as civil, criminal, juvenile, and domestic relations. All judges, circuit and associate, of the circuit courts have six-year terms.

Associate circuit judges hear lesser cases, civil or criminal, and all other matters that formerly were handled by magistrate or probate judges. In addition, they may be assigned additional cases as provided by the General Assembly (Section 17). They basically handle the minor cases that come before the circuit court system. The number of associate circuit judges for each county is determined by the General Assembly, but each county will have at least one resident associate circuit judge (Section 16). Circuit court judges must have been citizens of the United States for at least ten years and qualified voters of Missouri for three years preceding their selection, and they must be at least thirty years old and residents of the circuit for at least one year. Associate circuit judges shall be qualified voters of Missouri and residents of the county and at least twenty-five years of age (Section 21). Each circuit may have such municipal judges as provided by law and the necessary nonjudicial personnel assisting them. The selection, tenure, and compensation of such judges and such personnel are provided by the General Assembly or, in cities having a charter form of government, as provided by charter. A municipal judge may be a part-time judge except where prohibited by ordinance or charter of the municipality. A municipal judge hears and determines violations of municipal ordinances in one or more municipalities. There did develop a controversy in terms of the powers of a municipal judge relative to a city's human rights commission. The Supreme Court of Missouri ruled that it was the power of a municipal judge to determine violations of municipal ordinances. The power of the judge was based on the constitution, and a city charter could not violate the constitution.[10]

Associate circuit judges shall hear and determine violations of municipal ordinances in any municipality with a population of fewer than four hundred thousand within the circuit for which a municipal judge is not provided, or upon the request of the governing body of any municipality with a population of fewer than four hundred thousand within the circuit (Section 23). For municipalities of fewer than seventy-five hundred, the General Assembly has provided that a municipal judge need not be a lawyer, but attendance is required at a course of instruction prescribed by the supreme court.[11]

In addition to the sections that deal with the specific aspects of the various levels of courts, there are some general provisions that apply to the courts. Section 18 provides that all decisions, rules, and orders made by any administrative officer or body that are judicial or quasi judicial and affect private rights are subject to review by the courts under provisions established by the General Assembly. In cases where a hearing is required, the decision resulting from the hearing must be supported by competent and substantial evidence based on the whole record. Basically, what this requires is that administrative decisions of a judicial nature follow the essentials of due process that generally characterize judicial proceedings. The courts will exercise judicial review, and appeals, over these activities to ensure that proper procedure is followed.[12]

Section 20 provides directions regarding salaries of judges and provides that no judicial salary may be reduced during a judge's term of office. This is a traditional restriction, and it is designed to ensure judicial independence from the legislature. Also, a judge may neither receive additional compensation for any other public service nor participate in any legal business.

Section 24: Commission on Retirement, Removal, and Discipline

The constitution provides for a commission on retirement, removal, and discipline of judicial personnel. It is composed of two citizens, appointed by the governor, who are not members of the bar; two lawyers, appointed by the board of governors of the Missouri bar; one judge of the court of appeals, to be selected by a majority of the court of appeals judges; and one judge of the circuit courts, selected by a majority of the circuit judges (Section 24). The commission receives and investigates all requests and suggestions for retirement for disability and all complaints concerning misconduct of all judges and members of judicial commissions. The commission's investigation follows civil, not criminal, procedures, and its recommendations are only advisory.[13] Upon recommendation by an affirmative vote of at least four of the six members of the commission, the supreme court en banc, if it agrees, shall retire from office any judge or any member of any judicial commission who is found incapable of discharging the duties of his office with efficiency because of permanent sickness or physical or mental infirmity. Also, the supreme court shall—if it agrees with the recommendation of the commission—remove, suspend, discipline, or reprimand any judge of any court or any member of any judicial commission for the commission of a crime, or for misconduct, habitual drunkenness, willful neglect of duty, corruption in office, incompetence, or any offense involving moral turpitude or oppression. A judge is also disqualified from acting as a judicial officer while any of the following is pending: an indictment or information charging him in any court in the United States with a crime punishable as a felony under the laws of Missouri or of the United States, a recommendation to the supreme court by the commission for his removal or retirement, or articles of impeachment have been voted on by the House of Representatives.

The procedure for the removal or discipline of judges is seldom used, but matters have been brought before the commission, and it does offer a forum for the consideration of charges against judges without going through the difficult impeachment procedure.[14] The record of the commission over the past twenty-some years indicates that its recommendations are given much credibility by the supreme court. The commission has recommended five judges be removed from office, five judges be suspended from office without pay for periods of two weeks to ninety days, and one judge be reprimanded. The supreme court removed four judges and reduced one removal recommendation to a thirty-day suspension. The supreme court also suspended four judges and reduced one recommendation for suspension to a censure. The recommendation for one reprimand was not accepted by the supreme court.[15]

Section 25(a)–25(e): Judicial Selection

Judges in Missouri are chosen by three methods: partisan election, appointment, and appointment by the Nonpartisan or Missouri Plan. For the two upper levels of the court and the metropolitan courts the governor fills the vacancy by appointing one of three persons possessing the qualifications for the office, who shall have been nominated and whose names have been submitted to the governor by a nonpartisan judicial commission. If the governor fails to appoint any of the nominees within sixty days, the commission shall appoint one of the nominees (Section 25[a]). The constitution provides for the voters of the various judicial circuits to, by majority vote, elect to have the circuit and associate circuit judges appointed by the governor through the nonpartisan commission process; Green County did so recently. The question may be placed before the voters of a circuit if 10 percent of the legal voters of each county in the circuit voting for the office of governor at the last election shall file a petition (Section 25[b]).

The constitution defines the nonpartisan judicial commissions in Article V, Section 25(d). If for some reason there should arise a vacancy in the office of judge of the supreme court or of the court of appeals, a seven-member commission known as the Appellate Judicial Commission will make the nomination. The members of the commission select one of their number to serve as chair. For vacancies in the office of circuit judge or associate circuit judge of any circuit court using the nonpartisan court plan, a commission for each circuit known as the (number of the circuit) Circuit Judicial Commission will make the nomination. Each commission consists of five members: the chief judge of the district of the court of appeals within which the judicial circuit is located, two members of the bar who reside in the judicial circuit elected by their members, and two citizens, not members of the bar, from among the residents of the judicial circuit appointed by the governor. The members select one of their number to serve as chair.

The actual operation of the Nonpartisan (Missouri) Plan provides for the appointment by the governor from the list of three provided by the judicial commissions. Once the appointment is made, the judge takes office and holds it for a term ending on December 31, following the next general election after the expiration of twelve months in office. If the judge wishes to remain in office, he must file a declaration of candidacy for election to succeed himself. If a declaration is filed, his or her name will be submitted at the election, and the ballot shall read "Shall Judge [Here the name of the judge shall be inserted] of the [Here the title of the court shall be inserted] be retained in office? Yes/No." If a majority votes against him, the office becomes vacant as of December 31, following the election. If a majority supports him, the judge serves the term (Section 25[c]). In all the years that Missouri has used this plan, only two judges have not been retained (1942 and 1992). No appellate court judge has ever failed to receive a majority vote.

Most circuit and associate circuit judge positions outside the three major metropolitan areas are filled by partisan elections. Municipal judges in many rural areas are still appointed by the elected city officials.

Section 25(f): Prohibition of Political Activity

Political activity by judges is prohibited by Section 25(f). No judge of any court shall directly or indirectly make any contribution to or hold any office in a political party or organization or take part in any political campaign. In light of the recent U.S. Supreme Court case *Republican Party of Minnesota v. White*, there may be room for a more active political campaign in the retention elections of Missouri judges, since the court gave broader leeway for judges to discuss judicial issues as part of their campaigns.[16]

Section 26: Mandatory Retirement

Section 26 of the constitution provides for mandatory retirement of all judges other than municipal judges at the age of seventy years. However, it provides that any retired judge who wishes, and who is assigned by the supreme court, may act as a senior (temporary) judge of any court in the state and, when serving, shall have the same powers as an active judge. Mandatory retirement was challenged as a violation of the age-discrimination laws, but the national Supreme Court ruled that judges were involved in policy and therefore not covered.[17]

In our final words on the Missouri judiciary, we emphasize the fact that the court system that is provided for in the Missouri Constitution exists quite independently of the system of federal courts established by the national Constitution and by acts of Congress. There is no foundation whatsoever for the common notion that the highest state court is subordinate to the lowest federal court. True, certain classes of cases may begin in either the Missouri courts or the federal courts, and any case originating in the Missouri courts but involving determination of a right claimed under the national Constitution, laws, or treaties may be removed to or carried on appeal to the federal courts. Still, the great majority of cases coming before the Missouri courts do not raise any such "federal questions," but involve simply the adjudication of rights claimed under the Missouri Constitution, Missouri statutes, or the common law. Thus, in the overwhelming number of cases, the Missouri court system really is the court system of last resort for Missourians.

6

Miscellaneous Articles
Articles VI–XIII

Articles VI–XIII of the Missouri Constitution deal with a great variety of issues, topics as diverse as providing a framework for local governmental units such as counties and cities to the penalty for nepotism. Other subjects considered are taxation, education, railroads, corporations, banks, suffrage and elections, public officers, the manner in which amendments are proposed and adopted, and rules governing public employees. These represent the variety of powers left to the states by the U.S. Constitution that Missouri has chosen to specifically outline in its constitution.

Prior to a description of what the Constitution specifically says about each of these miscellaneous articles, we will, as has been our habit throughout this book, provide a description of the practical manifestation of the area of government. On some articles this will be short, reflecting their self-evident role; on others there will be more to say. For example, Article VI, "Local Governments," deals with the establishment of local governments. This topic will need a longer discussion because of the centrality of the topic to the understanding of Missouri government.

Article VI: Local Governments

Obviously, a major responsibility of the constitution is to establish the legal foundation for local governments: counties, townships, municipalities, and special districts. This can get complex if the state wants to be a close overseer. In order to give significant local control over local government organization, however, the constitution outlines the ability of most counties (population greater than eighty-five thousand) and larger cities, by popular vote, to set up their own government through the "charter" process. A charter is the equivalent of a local constitution in that it establishes, under general state guidelines, the type of government structure the local entity favors, the means by which it will operate, and the extent and powers of its elected officials. Most of the larger local governments are under charters; however, smaller units fall under general rules set by the constitution.

Counties

Counties are the fundamental subgovernmental units of the state. All parts of Missouri are within a county except for St. Louis. Because it was of significant size when the 1875 constitution was written, it had the geographical size and political influence to establish itself as the sole governmental unit for the city. Thus, though there is a St. Louis County that surrounds the city, the city is not within that county and must perform the duties of a county as well as those of a city. Paradoxically, then, St. Louis is both a city and a pseudocounty.

The Missouri Constitution outlines the foundations of county government, but leaves a great deal of the specifics to the General Assembly. For example, it allows for up to four classifications of counties but lets the legislature establish and define the qualifications for each classification. The basis for the classifications is not population size but rather the value of property assessment. The legislature periodically adjusts the values to redefine the four classifications; currently, the Class 1 counties (13 of them) have $600 million or more and Class 2 counties (6) have $460-$600 million in valuation. Class 3 counties have less than $460 million in valuation; there are 90 of them. There are only 2 poor Class 4 counties. In addition, the constitution allows for larger counties (population of eighty-five thousand in this case) to establish charter governments by vote of the citizens of the county. Of necessity, these are more complex systems and structures of government with singular, separately elected county executives as well as larger, district-based county legislatures. Only 4 counties are chartered: Jackson, St. Charles, St. Louis, and Greene, though the City of St. Louis is chartered for both city and county operation. This all means there are 114 counties plus St. Louis (city and county) in Missouri, the third-largest number in the nation.

Noncharter counties are directed to have a county government led by simply a three-person board—called county commissions. One commissioner is elected countywide and is the presiding commissioner, and the other two are elected from districts (North-South or East-West). In addition, separate county officials are independently elected to perform specific functions that are integral to what counties do. County governments provide a variety of functions that vary from county to county, especially between charter and noncharter counties. For smaller counties this includes primarily public safety (a sheriff), roads and bridges, running elections, and providing for a variety of public officials to perform specific functions (treasurer and county clerk, for example), outlined a bit later. Expanded services are performed by counties, depending on how much larger they are, in areas such as welfare, mass transportation, libraries, public health, water and air pollution control, water supply and sewage disposal, and parks and recreation. In the larger more urban counties, these functions and more are performed.

A basic function of all counties remains the chronicling of the legalities necessary to maintain a community. This means that counties are the core recorders of our lives—birth, death, marriage certification; divorce registration; real property registration; and tax liabilities. To these ends, counties and St. Louis elect officials to be responsible for particular areas of functioning within the county. The county sheriff is in charge of public safety, operating fundamentally outside of the incorporated areas of the county, and for various routine legal help to the courts. The county clerk keeps county records and, importantly, administers all elections under the broad supervision of the secretary of state. Because of historic corruption in St. Louis and Jackson County, though, a separate Election Commission made up equally of locally and state-chosen members administer elections. The county assessor is responsible for assessing real and personal property in the county for the establishing of property tax liabilities, and the county collector is responsible for actually collecting the tax moneys. The county treasurer receives all moneys (from local, state, and federal sources) going into all county funds and distributes it according to the decisions of the legal entities of the county. The county recorder of deeds is responsible for the certification and maintenance of records of all real property in the county. Class 2, 3, and 4 counties elect a county coroner responsible for certification of cause of death, but in all other counties (Class 1 and chartered) a medical examiner is appointed to perform this function.

The county public administrator is an interesting designation, since this office does not administer any government agency but rather oversees the estates of the unclaimed dead and of living children or incompetent individuals assigned to them by the courts. They tend to be paid partially by a percentage of the value of estates or by a set fee.

Two county-based officials are elected to perform judicial functions: the county prosecutor and the circuit clerk to the associate judge of the county. Sometimes in smaller counties some of the official responsibilities are combined for efficiency's sake. For example, Nodaway County combines the county collector's and county treasurer's duties into one office.

Interestingly enough, the constitution is concerned with compensation for some county, and indeed city, officials. It gives the General Assembly leeway to set salaries or salary limits or the mechanisms for setting salaries. Thus, some counties have a "Salary Commission" that sets the salary of key elected officials in the county, though the legislature sets limits.

Townships are subdivisions of counties made available for the convenience of rural counties in earlier times. Only twenty-one counties have townships, fourteen of them in the northwest corner of the state, whose major responsibility is town-to-market roads (usually the gravel ones).

Cities and Towns

The constitution follows the pattern used for counties by establishing the ability of the state legislature to provide both for classification of municipalities with separate limitations and for charter cities with more "home rule." These latter have flexibility in choosing government-organization type and operations upon vote of their citizens.

Generally, the legislature has limited villages, 500 people or fewer, to having only a board of trustees (or city council, some call themselves) form of government with five or nine members on the board. The commissioners divide the administrative departments among themselves to oversee the operation of government: one member of the commission or council is often designated "mayor" but has only ceremonial responsibilities. Larger entities, cities and towns more than 500–2,999 designated Class 4 cities, have some variation of one of two forms of government: a mayor-council form or a council-manager form. Class 3 cities (3,000–29,999) can have the same options with a bit more flexibility. In 1975 the statute for Class 1 and 2 cities was repealed, since most have home-rule charters.

The *mayor-council* form of local government elects a mayor separately from the city council, creating an executive and a legislative council. A strong form of mayor-council gives the mayor veto powers, direction of the departmental units of administration, and power to submit the budget. Weaker forms eliminate one or more of these three powers and leave them to the council. Some mayors, though executives, are placed within the city council and preside over it.

The *council-manager* form of city government is based on an elected city council. This council then appoints a professional manager to run the city's departments—hiring and firing department heads and personnel. The role is of an unelected executive who focuses on administration. This form is supposed to bring efficiency and lessen decisions based on politics. Although this may or may not happen, it does provide for a clear responsibility for the running of the city by the professional manager. The council usually elects one of its members to preside and be the ceremonial mayor but with no additional powers accruing to the mayor. Many charter cities mix the two basic systems by electing a mayor separately in a fundamentally council-manager format and assign the position some degree of powers. Others have a mayor-council form and still hire a professional administrator to run the city on a day-to-day basis.

It should be remembered that the functions of the municipalities are governed by state law with limitations and responsibilities assigned by that law. Governance at the local level is dependent for all its powers and responsibilities upon the constitution and the state's ability to regulate as it chooses. The distribution of powers called federalism gives sovereign powers to states and none to local governments.

The last category of local governments is a large category of narrow-function entities called *special districts.* These are just as they appear, districts set up within the county or city to perform specific tasks, often a task not performed by the county or city. Thus, rural water, ambulance, and even sewer districts are common special districts outside of towns and cities. Within cities a variety of special purposes can be established from parks and recreation districts to special business districts to help pay for particular improvements in business neighborhoods. These are governmental units with taxing powers, narrow legislative responsibilities, and elected officials to run them. They are a popular way to fill in areas of responsibilities that often fall through the cracks of the larger traditional governmental units. We do not want to go into depth with all the specifics outlined in the Constitution, so as you read through the following overview, note the particulars that the Constitution contains as a means of conferring as well as limiting the powers and responsibilities of local governments.

Sections 1–22: County and Municipal Government

This article begins with a consideration of counties; it recognizes counties as legal subdivisions of the state and provides for their continuation unless their organization is changed by the procedures authorized by the constitution (Sections 1–5). The procedure for consolidation of two or more counties requires a majority vote of the qualified electors in each county affected. The same procedure would be required if a county were to be divided or have some portion of it removed. A county could be dissolved by a vote of two-thirds of the qualified electors of the county. County seats may be changed by the same two-thirds vote, but this vote may be taken only once every five years (Section 6). Section 7 provides that each county that does not frame and adopt its own charter, or adopt an alternative form of county government, will be managed by three elected officials. The voters in each county could reduce the number to one or two as provided by the General Assembly.

Section 8 provides the framework for the organization and classification of counties. The number of classes is not to exceed four, and the organization and powers of each class are defined by general laws so that all counties within the same class possess the same powers and are governed by the same restrictions. Section 8 was amended in 1995 to allow any county having more than eighty-five thousand residents to frame, adopt, and amend a charter for its own government (amendment placed in Section 18[a]). In addition, any county that had been a first-class county for at least two years would be eligible for a charter form of government. Counties with charter government would be separate and not subject to the classification system established by Section 8. The Supreme Court of Missouri has ruled that statutory provisions that were intended to apply only to a particular county, favoring or punishing them, violated Section 8.[1]

The counties not covered by the exceptions for charter governments (Section 18) are divided into four classes based on their taxable base; thus, the powers and responsibilities of each county are based on its total assessed valuation.[2] When inflation pushes a county into another class, increasing its financial responsibility without any corresponding increase in its real financial abilities, problems develop. To counteract such problems, the General Assembly periodically upgrades its classification scheme.

Section 9 allows the General Assembly to provide alternative forms of county government for counties of any particular class. Often the constitution leaves some flexibility to the discretion of the legislature.

The terms of county and city offices cannot exceed four years, and the compensation of county officers—except for counties that operate under a charter form of government—is prescribed by law or established by each county as provided by the General Assembly (Sections 10 and 11). In this regard the General Assembly has authorized a county salary commission for each unchartered county. The commission establishes the compensation for each office, but there is a maximum compensation allowable under state law.[3]

Sections 11–13 provide some direction as to the compensation of county officers in regard to fees and salaries. The General Assembly has the major responsibility for determining where the revenue collected by fees will be allocated. Section 14 provides for the joint participation (cooperation) by counties in certain activities such as purchasing, construction, and the maintenance of hospitals and road machinery or use of any other county property. This can be accomplished by a majority vote of the qualified electors in each county affected. Counties may also join in the employment of any county officer or employee common to each of the counties. This too must by approved by a vote in each county.

Section 15 allows for the General Assembly to provide the organization and classification of cities and towns.[4] Again, as is true for counties, the number of such classes is not to exceed four, and the powers of each class are defined by the General Assembly so that all cities of the same class shall have the same powers and be subject to the same restrictions.

The relationship of different governmental units is also considered. Sections 16 and 17 recognize the need that different political subdivisions of the state have to contract and cooperate with other political subdivisions; such activities are allowed, subject to state law. Consolidation and separation of municipalities and other political subdivisions are allowed, but again, the process is subject to state law and involves public approval.

In addition to the general classification of local governments, Article VI provides for special charter governments (Section 18[a–r]). Any county having more than eighty-five thousand inhabitants may frame, adopt, and amend a charter for its own government. This charter must provide for the form of county government; the number, kind, manner of selection, terms of office, and salaries of the county officers; and the exercise of all powers and duties of counties and county officers prescribed by the constitution and laws of the state. Taxation under a county charter would still be limited to the extent of authorization under the constitution or state law. Section 18 also spells out the method whereby a county may move to a charter government, including petitions for charter commission, the charter commission, and the manner of the special election. A charter must be approved in a special election by a majority vote of the qualified voters of the county. The procedure for amending charters is also provided. If a charter is defeated, it may not be resubmitted to the voters until two years after its defeat. Section 18 was substantially amended in 1994 and 1995 in response to the problems the General Assembly was experiencing in providing legislation that would be responsive to the problems of the urban counties.

A charter form of government for cities is described in Sections 19–22. Cities having more than five thousand inhabitants, and any other cities that may be provided by law, are eligible for a charter form of government. Again, the procedure is outlined carefully in terms of electing a charter commission, amendments, petitions, and the special election. This ability of a city to adopt its own charter and to a large extent define its own powers (within the limits of state legislation) is often referred to as "home rule" and is thought to be much preferred to the rather limited authority allowed most cities under the general class legislation. A city that adopts a charter for its own government would have all powers that the General Assembly has authority to confer upon any city, provided such powers are consistent with the constitution and are not limited or denied, either by the charter so adopted or by statute.[5] Such a city will, in addition to its home rule powers, have all powers conferred by law. Despite this, few cities in Missouri have taken advantage of these provisions. Apparently, citizens prefer their city governments to operate with rather limited power.

Sections 23–29: Finances

Article VI deals with local government finances, and, as was the case in dealing with the financial limitations of state government, the provisions are quite detailed in describing the powers of local government. Section 13 prohibits the ownership of stock in any corporation or association by any political subdivision. Also, there can be no lending of credit or granting of public money or anything of value to aid any corporation, association, or individual. A city may borrow money to purchase, construct, extend, or improve plants to be leased or otherwise disposed of pursuant to law to private persons or corporations for manufacturing, warehousing, and industrial development. This, however, must be subject to all provisions of the constitution and be approved by a two-thirds vote of the qualified electors voting in that jurisdiction (Section 23). This provision has been challenged, and the general rule, which the Supreme Court of Missouri has established, is that a private project that may reap substantial benefit from the use of public money would not violate this constitutional provision as long as the measures adopted represented the least-expensive method of achieving the appropriate governmental objective.[6] Section 23 also places a limit on the size of the indebtedness relative to the value of taxable tangible property in the affected jurisdiction.

Other requirements deal with annual budgets, reports, and audits of local governments (Section 24). Sections 25–27 detail the use of credit and the grant of public funds by local governments in terms of pensions and retirement plans for employees and the limitation on indebtedness of local governments without popular vote and a limitation of the indebtedness of local government even if authorized by popular vote. In addition, indebtedness for specific purposes, such as public improvements and municipally owned water and light plats, is stipulated. Restrictions on the use of revenue bonds for industrial development, utilities, and airports are also included. A "revenue bond" is defined as a bond for which neither the interest nor the principal is an indebtedness or obligation of the issuing county, city, or incorporated town or village. In effect, the revenue bond's target will pay for the retirement of the bond's debt.

Sections 28–29 allow for "refunding bonds" and restrict the use of all borrowed money to the purpose for which it was borrowed or to repayment of the debt.

Sections 30–33: City and County of St. Louis

The last sections of Article VI deal with the city and county of St. Louis. Direction is given as to the relationship of the city of St. Louis and the county of St. Louis in terms of intergovernmental relations between the two entities, and provision is made for a board to provide leadership and direction on duties as outlined by the constitution (Section 30). An example of the application of this clause was a challenge made to a rate adjustment in property taxes affecting both St. Louis City and St. Louis County. The Supreme Court of Missouri ruled that to treat the political subdivisions of St. Louis City and St. Louis County differently for rate adjustments after assessment was unconstitutional.[7]

Section 31 recognizes the city of St. Louis as both a city and a county and requires the city to operate under its charter subject to changes and amendments provided by the constitution or by law. A method for revising the charter is also provided (Sections 32 and 33). A dispute developed over the constitutional provision that allows St. Louis to reorganize its governmental structure by popular vote on a plan put forth by a board of freeholders. Freeholders had been interpreted to mean someone who owned land, and the city maintained that only landowners could be elected to the board. The Supreme Court of Missouri refused to allow this interpretation, ruling that it constituted a form of discrimination that violated the equal protection clause of the U.S. Fourteenth Amendment. The term freeholder was ordered stricken from the state constitution.[8]

Article VII: Public Officers

Sections 1–4: Impeachment and Removal from Office

This article deals with public officers and begins with a discussion of impeachment (Sections 1–4). All elective executive officials of the state as well as all judges of the supreme court, court of appeals, and circuit courts are liable to impeachment for committing a crime, misconduct, habitual drunkenness, willful neglect of duty, corruption of office, incompetence, or any offense involving moral turpitude or oppression in office (Section 1). The House of Representatives has the sole power of impeachment, which means that the House must make the charges. All impeachments are to be tried before the Supreme Court of Missouri, except that of the governor or a member of the supreme court, who is to be tried by a special commission of seven eminent jurists selected by the Senate (Section 2). The trial is not in the Senate, as is the case in the U.S. Constitution. Having been found guilty, the official is removed from office and is liable for any other punishment appropriate to the officer's behavior (Section 3).

In 1994 the Supreme Court of Missouri had an opportunity to apply these provisions in a case that involved the office of secretary of state.[9] Secretary of State Judith Moriarty had been convicted in circuit court of a misdemeanor. The supreme court found, as the circuit court had, that Moriarty had failed to prevent and failed to repudiate conduct that created a false declaration of candidacy. Moriarty's son had been given privileges and special treatment not available to any other person seeking public office. The supreme court in its written decision stated that its role in the impeachment process was that of a court and not a substitute political body. Conviction would depend on actual misconduct as the law defined it. The definition of misconduct would be the doing of an unlawful act, doing a lawful act in an unlawful manner, or failing to perform an act required by law. It would not include errors in judgment, acts done in good faith, or good faith exercise of discretion. The standard of proof required to convict was clear and convincing evidence was presented, and so she was removed. All officers that are not subject to impeachment may be removed from office in the manner and for causes as provided by law (Section 4).

Section 5–7: Election and Appointment

Section 5 deals with elections. It provides that in contested elections for governor, lieutenant governor, and other executive offices, the supreme court shall decide the winner. When other public officers of the state are involved in contested elections, the determinations are by lower courts of law, and the General Assembly is to provide by general law the court and judge by whom the several classes of election contests shall be tried.

Article VII, Section 6, provides a penalty for nepotism. It states that any public officer or employee who by virtue of his or her office or employment names or appoints to public office or employment any relative within the fourth degree—by blood relationship or marriage—shall thereby forfeit the office or employment. This becomes quite complicated, but it basically would mean that a public officer could not appoint anyone more closely related than a great-grandnephew or great-grandniece, first cousin once removed, or a great-granduncle or great-grandaunt. The antinepotism provision makes no exception for public officials who appoint relatives to serve in public office without pay.[10]

Section 7 gives to the General Assembly the power to determine the qualifications for the appointment of officers, subject, of course, to constitutional provisions.

Sections 8–14: Qualifications for Office

Section 8 deals with some of these constitutional provisions by providing that no person shall be elected or appointed to any civil or military office who is not a U.S. citizen and who shall not have resided in Missouri for one year preceding his or her election or appointment, except that the residency requirement may be waived in cases of appointment to administrative positions requiring technical or specialized skill or knowledge. The governor often appoints out-of-state cabinet members on the basis of this section. The holding of any federal employment disqualifies any Missouri employment except for reserve armed service personnel (Section 9).

Before taking office, all civil and military officers must take an oath to support the Constitution of the United States and that of the state of Missouri and to conduct themselves faithfully in office (Section 11). Section 10 provides a strong statement regarding sexual discrimination. It states that no person shall be disqualified from holding office in this state because of gender. This provision goes back to the constitution of 1875, Article VIII, Section 1. The present version was adopted in August 1921.

Tenure in office is the subject of Section 12; it provides that, subject to constitutional provisions, all officers shall serve for the term of the office and until such time as their successors are duly elected or appointed. Some commission appointees hang on for a year or more if the governor is slow to appoint a replacement.

There also is a quite common governmental restriction contained in Section 13, which states that compensation of state, county, and municipal officers shall not be increased during their terms of office, nor shall the term of any officer be extended. This is designed to prevent officers from enriching themselves while in office and maintaining themselves in office without a vote of the people.

Last, the legislature must provide the cost of any increase in retirement benefits for officials publicly before enactment (Section 14).

Article VIII: Suffrage and Elections

Section 1 requires that general elections be held on the Tuesday following the first Monday in November of each even-numbered year, unless a different day is fixed by law with two-thirds of all members of each house assenting. Voter qualifications are also defined. All citizens of the United States over the age of eighteen who are residents of Missouri and of the political subdivision in which they wish to vote are entitled to vote in all elections. Voters need to have resided in their political subdivision for thirty days preceding the election in which they wish to vote. Those who may be disqualified from voting by law would be those who have a guardian by reason of mental incapacity, those who are involuntarily confined in a mental institution, or persons convicted of felonies or crimes connected with the exercise of the right of suffrage (Section 2). Section 4 says that voters cannot be arrested coming to or from voting except in cases of treason, felony, or breach of the peace.

The secrecy of the ballot is also ensured. All election officers are sworn not to disclose how any voter voted. However, election officers may be required to testify, and the ballots cast may be opened, examined, counted, and received as evidence in cases of contested elections, grand jury investigations, and the trial of all civil or criminal cases in which the violations of any law relating to elections—including primary elections—are under investigation or at issue (Section 3).

Section 5 allows the General Assembly to require registration of voters, and the General Assembly has so required; though earlier in its history the legislature had exempted rural citizens, this was changed to include these areas. In a 2006 case the court defined the right to vote by ruling that the right to vote was a fundamental right and therefore subject to strict scrutiny. Thus, a statute requiring a photo ID for qualified and registered voters was deemed by the supreme court, again in 2006, not to be tailored to meet the state's compelling interests and thus violated equal protection of the law.[11] If there are irregularities in an election based on voter qualifications, a new election could be ordered.[12]

Residency for voting purposes is retained by those individuals who are absent from their Missouri residence while engaged in the civil or military service of Missouri or the United States or while a student at any institution (Section 6). The right of absentee voting is also provided by general law for all elections (Section 7).

In 1966 voters by initiative added to this article (skipping numbers 8–14) Sections 15–22, which outline a complex description of a demand for U.S. congressional term limits. In short, they set the term limits at three terms if the national Constitution is amended to allow it. In addition, it called upon congressional candidates to pledge themselves to limit their terms to two. Although interesting, there has been no substantive effect of these sections.

Article IX: Education

Education is a vital role of state and local governments, and this is reflected in the use of a separate article for the purpose of describing this role in Missouri. Free public education is guaranteed here, meaning primary and secondary education, and its financing is to be secured. This education is, of course, actually provided by local school districts within counties, townships, or cities throughout the state. These are special district governments run by boards who provide for the administration, the teachers, and the financing of the school districts through local property taxes. The state, in addition, must provide at least 25 percent of its income for free public education.

Sections 1–3: Free Public Schools and Administration

Section 1 begins with a strong statement concerning the importance of education: "A general diffusion of knowledge and intelligence being essential to the preservation of the rights and liberties of the people, the General Assembly shall establish and maintain free public schools for the gratuitous instruction of all persons in this state within ages not in excess of twenty-one years as prescribed by law." The possibility of specific schools for adult education is allowed, but the funds must not be from ordinary school revenues.

Section 2 provides for a state Board of Education and a commissioner of education and details the appointment by the governor and Senate and their operation.

Section 3 directs that there will be annual support by the state for free public schools, and if there is a deficiency in providing for funds to sustain the schools for at least eight months, the General Assembly may provide funds to overcome such deficiency. In no case shall there be set apart less than 25 percent of the state revenue, exclusive of interest and sinking fund, to be applied annually to the support of the free public schools.

Racial discrimination in employment of teachers is prohibited by Section 3 by the requirement that no school district shall receive any portion of state revenue if it permits differences in wages of teachers having the same training and experience because of race or color.

Sections 4–7: School Funding

Sections 4–7 concern restrictions on indebtedness and the use of income in educational operations. These sections continue the thrust of constitutional restrictions on finances by detailing how school funds are to be administered. Section 4 provides direction in terms of state obligations toward the handling of public school funds. Not surprisingly, public school funding has been the source of much litigation. The supreme court has been asked, for example, to determine the power of the General Assembly to allocate funds on a number of occasions. The latest was in 2009 when the court applied the "rational basis" review to rule that the school funding formula did not violate Missouri's equal protection clause. The providing of more state funds to school districts with fewer local funds

did not violate a fundamental right. There is no constitutional requirement to provide equal spending per student in districts throughout the
state.[13] The state is obligated to ensure the availability of school funds,
and, if the funds are to be invested, directs that they can be invested only
in registered bonds of the United States or the state, bonds of school districts of the state, or bonds or other securities that are fully guaranteed by
the United States.

The protection of public school funds also is the subject of Section 5.
It requires that all funds available for public schools must be securely invested and sacredly preserved for establishing and maintaining free public schools. Section 6 basically repeats Section 5, but this time the funds
to be protected are funds available for the state university (University of
Missouri). County and township school funds are the topic of Section 7,
and again, the thrust is to provide direction in terms of use of these funds
to ensure that the funds are protected and are used for educational purposes. The great concern over funding of education is also evident from a
requirement in Section 7 that the proceeds of all penalties, forfeitures, and
fines collected for any breach of the penal laws of the state, and the net
proceeds from the sale of stray domestic animals, should be available for
school purposes and none other.[14]

Section 8 reinforces the near-absolute prohibition of the use of public
funds for religious institutions stated in Section 7 of the Missouri Bill of
Rights. In this case no local governmental entity, including school districts
can give any kind of aid to church-related schools.

Section 9: The University of Missouri

Section 9 deals with the University of Missouri and provides for its governing system: a board of curators, consisting of nine members appointed
by the governor with the consent of the Senate. Section 9(b) states that the
General Assembly shall adequately maintain the state university and such
other educational institutions as it may deem necessary.

Section 10: Public Libraries

Free public libraries are dealt with in Section 10; it is the policy of the state
to promote the establishment and development of free public libraries and
to accept the obligation of their support by the state and its subdivisions
and municipalities in such manners as may be provided by law. But there
is no obligatory support.

Article X: Taxation

Sections 1–3: Taxing Powers

Sections 1 and 2 of this article define who has the taxing power and for what uses taxes may be put. In general, the General Assembly may use its taxing power for state purposes. Counties and other political subdivisions may exercise such taxing power as the General Assembly may grant them for their respective governmental purposes, but there is included a prohibition of the delegation of any of these taxing powers by local governments.

Political subdivision as defined by Section 15 of Article X includes townships, cities, towns, villages, schools, road drainage, sewer and levee districts, and any other public subdivision, public corporation, or public quasi-corporation having the power to tax. Government is defined by the power to tax.

Section 3 provides that taxes may be levied and collected for public purposes only and that taxes must be uniform upon the same class or subclass of subjects within the territorial limits of the authority levying the tax. The General Assembly makes the classifications for tax purposes. The constitutional standard is that there must be adequate justification for the classification scheme.[15] An example of this was a controversy over the taxing of private but not public pensions. The Supreme Court of Missouri ruled that this distinction was reasonable given the objectives of the legislature.[16] The test applied by the court in regard to the uniformity clause is the same as the rational-basis test. Under this test, a statute will be sustained if the state legislature reasonably could have concluded that the challenged classification would promote a legitimate state purpose.[17]

Section 4: Classification of Property

Classification of property is the subject of Section 4. It provides different classification of property for tax purposes: Class 1, real property; Class 2, tangible personal property; and Class 3, intangible personal property. The General Assembly is allowed to make further classifications within Classes 2 and 3 based solely on the nature and characteristics of the property. In addition, subclasses are provided for property in Class 1. The three subclasses are residential property, agricultural and horticultural property, and utility, industrial, commercial, railroad, and all other property not included in Classes 1 and 2.

Section 4 further states that land in Subclass 2 may, by general law, be assessed for tax purposes on its productive capability. The same percentage of value shall be applied to all properties within any subclass, but no class or subclass shall have a percentage of its true value in money in excess of 33.33 percent. This represents the fundamental directive on property-tax limitations in the constitution.

Sections 5–9: Relief from Taxation

Other aspects of Article X deal with such matters as what level of government is to assess, levy, collect, and receive the receipts from certain types of taxes. Property tax, for example, is a county responsibility. Income tax is discussed in terms of the power of the General Assembly to set the rate and define income. Section 5 provides for taxation of railroads. Section 6 has an extensive listing of property that the General Assembly may make exempt from taxation. Examples would be all property of the state, counties, and other political subdivisions and property not held for private or corporate profit—such as religious, educational, and charitable purposes. Also included is a procedure whereby the revenue lost by the exemption could be compensated for by allowing an increase in the tax on certain other properties. The ability to offer tax relief to certain type of properties is an important power of government. Examples of this use would be providing relief for projects dealing with land clearance and redevelopment. A tax abatement for these activities has been allowed under this provision.[18] Also, certain charitable activities are supported through tax exemptions.[19]

Section 6 also deals with other possibilities for the General Assembly to provide additional exemptions from property tax. A homestead exemption is provided, which allows the General Assembly to provide that a portion of the assessed valuation of real property actually occupied by the owner or owners as a homestead be exempted from the payment of taxes. The General Assembly could provide tax credits or rebates in lieu of or in addition to such an exemption. But the General Assembly must provide for restitution to the political subdivisions of revenues lost. Also provided is comparable financial relief to persons who are not owners of homesteads but who rent their homes.

Sections 7 and 8 provide for relief from taxation for forestlands and blighted areas and place a limit on state tax on real and tangible personal property. Section 9 protects private property from being taken or sold for the payment of the corporate debt of a municipal corporation.

Sections 10–15: Local Governments and Taxation

Section 10 prevents the General Assembly from raising local taxes for local purposes but provides that the funds collected for state purposes may be allocated to counties and other political subdivisions as state aid for local purposes. In addition, it recognizes the power of the General Assembly to control the rates of levy and all property taxes of all political subdivisions.

Section 11 limits the taxing power of local governments' rates, and provides for tax-rate increases by popular vote. In 1988 voters approved an amendment that required a four-seventh majority to approve bond issues for constructing and improving schools, roads, bridges, and job-development projects on municipal, primary, and general election days. The two-thirds majority was retained for all other election days. The provision on election days was put in to prevent the submitting of bond proposals at elections where few people vote. This amendment was a major change, since there had been numerous unsuccessful attempts to change the two-thirds vote requirement in the past. The two-thirds majority requirement had made it exceedingly difficult to increase the tax rate.

Section 12 deals with additional tax rates for county roads and bridges and details under what conditions additional taxes may be levied. Section 13 limits the sale of property for the payment of taxes in terms of the judicial procedure that must be followed.

The Equalization Commission is provided for in Section 14. Its major duty is to provide a forum for appeals from local assessments in individual cases and to correct any assessment that is shown to be unlawful, unfair, arbitrary, or capricious. Since property tax is a major source of revenue, this commission, with its supervisory power over all assessments of real property, is in an important position in regard to providing a fair system of taxation. Section 15 defines political subdivisions as any "public subdivision, public corporation, or public quasi-corporation having the power to tax."

What can be concluded from the foregoing sections is that state and local officials must look carefully at the constitution (and consequent laws) to determine what they can and cannot do in the area of taxation. The constitution simply provides a bevy of limitations.

Sections 16–24: The Hancock Amendment

Perhaps the most important restrictions on the General Assembly's financial powers is contained in Sections 16–24 of Article X—commonly called the "Hancock Amendment," after its main sponsor. These provisions, which require tax and spending ceilings, are extremely complicated and continue to cause much confusion in their application.[20] The general thrust, however, is that total state revenue increases are tied to the annual rate that personal income has increased in the state since the adoption of the amendment. If the state collects funds in excess of the permissible amount, the state must refund the surplus to taxpayers. In fiscal 1995, the state exceeded the revenue ceiling. However, there was still confusion as to the exact application of the amendment since the Office of Administration, Division of Budget and Planning, determined the refund to be $147 million and the State Auditor's Office determined it to be $617 million.[21] The base year for determining total state revenue under the tax-lid provision is fiscal year 1980–1981. The revenues included would be all general and special revenue and all license fees as defined in the budget message of the governor. Federal funds were excluded. Also, the Supreme Court of Missouri ruled that "total state revenue" did not include the opening fund balance.[22] The personal income of Missourians would include total income received by persons in Missouri from all sources. The source of this figure would be the U.S. Department of Commerce (Section 17).

The tax lid is determined by computing the percentage increase in the personal income of Missouri residents for any calendar year. If, for example, there had been a 4 percent increase in the personal income, any increase in state revenue would be considered in relation to this 4 percent limit. Beginning in 1981–1982 and for each year thereafter, the General Assembly could not impose taxes of any kind that, together with all other revenue of the state, would exceed a revenue limit based on the increase in the personal income of state residents. If the total revenue of the state exceeded the revenue limit by 1 percent or more, the excess amount would have to be refunded to taxpayers based on taxes paid as reported on the Missouri state income tax forms (Section 18). This revenue limit is also a limit on state spending, since the state must have a balanced budget. No expense of state government could be incurred that would exceed the sum of this revenue limit plus federal funds and any surplus from a previous year (Section 20).

Section 19 provides for exceptions regarding revenue limits. It states that the limits can be exceeded only if the following conditions are met: the governor requests the General Assembly to declare an emergency; the request must be specific as to the nature of the emergency, the dollar amount of the emergency, and the method by which the emergency will be funded; and the General Assembly declares an emergency in accordance with the specifics of the governor's request by a two-thirds vote in each house.

A major provision (Section 21) affecting local governments is the requirement that local governments are forbidden to increase taxes or fees without a vote of their constituents. A problem for local governments was the definition of fees.[23] The General Assembly attempted to solve this problem by defining the term *increasing* as used in Section 22 of Article X when referring to any license or fee of any county or other political subdivision as not meaning adjustments in the level of any license or fee necessary to maintain funding of a program.[24] This would eliminate the need for a vote on most fee increases. The supreme court provided some clarity (or confusion) to this section in a 1993 case. The question dealt with the legality of a sewer district's increase in charges without voter approval. Five questions were used to determine whether the sewer charge was subject to a public vote: When is the fee paid? Who pays the fee? Is the amount of the fee to be paid affected by the level of goods or services provided to the fee payee? Is the government providing a service or a good? Has the activity been historically and exclusively provided by the government? After answering questions 1 and 3 as indicating the fee was subject to a public vote, 2 and 4 as indicating that the fees were not covered, and finding that the evidence on question 5 was inconclusive, the court ruled that when the court was uncertain as to the need for a public vote, the court must rule in favor of the right of the people to vote on a proposed increase in the sewer charge. The burden was on the government to demonstrate that the charges were permissible without a vote. In this case the subdivision had not been able to demonstrate clearly that the sewer charges were not subject to a vote. The conclusion that sewer service charges are a tax, license, or fee was reinforced by a 1995 case where the court stated that it would continue to use the five-pronged test to distinguish between the taxes, licenses, and fees that require voter approval and fees not subject to voter approval.[25]

The taxation sections also required that property taxes, other local taxes, and state taxation could not be increased above the limits contained in Sections 17–24 without a vote of the people. Also, the state is prohibited from requiring any new or expanded activity by counties or political subdivisions without full state financing and from shifting the tax burden to counties and other political subdivisions.[26] These provisions could be avoided under emergency conditions or when it is to guarantee the repayment of voter-approved bonded indebtedness (Section 16).

Article XI:
Corporations, Railroads, and Banks

Sections 1–8: Corporations

This article begins by defining a corporation and requiring the corporation to be organized only under general laws (Sections 1 and 2). This is consistent with the prohibition against the General Assembly's passing special laws.

Section 3 provides that the exercise of the police power of the state shall never be allowed to permit corporations to infringe the equal rights of individuals or the general well-being of the state. This has never been a major issue in terms of legislative power, but it is an interesting example of a populist attitude. This section, like many others, was taken from the constitution of 1875.

Corporations are also made subject to the right of eminent domain, and the right of trial by jury is preserved in all claims of compensation when the rights of any corporation are affected by any exercise of eminent domain (Section 4). The election of directors or managers of any corporation is also subject to direction. The general thrust is to protect the power of the shareholders (Section 6). (Section 5 was repealed in 1988.)

The issue of stocks and bonds or other obligations of the corporations is also subject to restrictions: no stockholder, subscriber to stock, or corporation shall be individually liable in any amount in excess of the amount originally subscribed on such stock (Sections 7 and 8).

Sections 9–12: Railroads

Railroads are declared to be common carriers and subject to laws enacted to correct abuses and to prevent unjust discrimination and extortion in the rates of freights and passenger tariffs on all railroads in the state (Section 9). Section 10 also provides that any railroad corporation organized under Missouri law that is consolidated with any railroad corporation organized under the laws of other states is subject to the jurisdiction of Missouri courts in all matters. Local authorities are given the right to consent to the construction and operation of a street railroad within any city, town, or village or on any public highway (Section 11). Section 12 requires that no discrimination in charges or facilities in transportation be made between transportation corporations and individuals or in favor of either.

Section 13: Banks

This one-sentence section simply excludes the state from creating or owning any state bank.

Article XII: Amendments

This article provides that the General Assembly may propose amendments at any time by a majority of members of each house, or amendments may be proposed by initiative. The amendment must be published in newspapers throughout the state. The amendment vote would be at the next general election or at a special election called by the governor. If the majority of votes cast favor the amendment, it would take effect thirty days after the election (Sections 1 and 2). In a 1991 case, the Supreme Court of Missouri voided a statute that required a sample initiative petition be submitted to the secretary of state one year before the initiative would be placed before the voters. The ruling stated that sample initiative petitions may be presented to the secretary of state at any time during the periods between elections.[27]

A proposed amendment may contain only one amended and revised article or one new article and shall contain only one subject and matters properly connected therewith. The exact meaning of the one-subject requirement has been the source of controversy. The Supreme Court of Missouri has ruled that, in terms of this requirement, if an amendment deals with several articles of the constitution, it is suspect.[28]

Article XIII:
Public Employees in the Constitution

Sections 1–2: Medical Benefits

This is a very short article (two sections) and deals with public employee medical benefits. The thrust of the article is to allow the General Assembly to provide health insurance benefits for officers and employees of the state and their dependents. The General Assembly may authorize other political subdivisions to provide health insurance for their officers.

Conclusion

An Evolving Document

The Missouri Constitution has come a long way since its first manifestation in 1820. Then the only elected officials at the state level were the governor, the lieutenant governor, and the General Assembly. Few limits were placed on the legislature except to maintain the institution of slavery. Ironically, the post–Civil War constitution of 1865 could be characterized by its punishment of the Southern sympathizers while at the same time denying the vote to the newly freed slaves (negated by the U.S. Thirteenth Amendment in late 1865).

It took the constitution of 1875 to correct these oversights and to begin the progress toward a more specific document designed to place more limits on state government. Maximum tax rates were set, segregation was mandatory, and state income had to provide for public schools. The course of politics led to demands for more public services so that the executive branch began to grow without constitutional structures mandated. Growth and social changes led to demands for a constitutional convention, and the post–World War II world was projected to be significantly different from the past. The constitution needed rethinking.

The bipartisan convention used a great deal of the fundamentals of the 1875 constitution, in the Missouri Bill of Rights, for example, but added significant restrictions on government while defining its structure more particularly. It stayed long, then.[1]

Besides this bumpy history and the continuity of the 1875 constitution, the 1945 Missouri Constitution has continued to reflect the influence of the national Constitution, national laws, and U.S. Supreme Court decisions. In addition, through the years the document has been changed by many amendments, and it has also been subject to interpretation through the

Missouri court process. The document is always changing and certainly has always been affected by the political environment within which it operated. This is no less true today than in earlier times.

In an article published in 1962, prior to the vote calling for a constitutional convention, it was argued that there was again a need for substantial revision of the constitution. The 1945 constitution was compared to a model state constitution proposed by constitutional experts, and it was concluded that there were major difficulties with the constitution. First, it was observed that the language of the constitution was not clear and understandable. Second, the document was long and inflexible. Third, the constitution was much too specific and needed to be changed to deal mostly with fundamentals.[2] Despite these arguments, Missourians did not approve a constitutional convention in 1962, nor has it in consequent twenty-year votes.

The 1945 constitution reflects a desire for limited government at both the state and the local levels, and this objective appears to continue to reflect the thinking of Missouri voters.[3] This certainly has been the case in both the use of amendments and court interpretations. A reflection of this resonates through what has happened with the Missouri Bill of Rights. From the addition of the victims' rights amendment to interpretation of the concealed weapons phraseology in the document, the courts have now become more important than ever as a source of individual protection. The thematic distrust of government has always been indicated in the detail of the document, and this has been reinforced by the adoption of a number of amendments that have placed additional restrictions on government activity. Taxation issues illustrate this point dramatically, especially the "Hancock Amendment." The detail of the document enhances the role for the courts in Missouri by allowing them to interpret these various restrictions. Even so, not to be left out, the courts are also subject to limitations. The specificity of clauses makes them less subject to broad interpretation, and the ease of amending the document, even by the direct process of initiative, means that there is a strong check against judicial lawmaking.

Robert F. Karsch, a longtime observer and expert on Missouri government, stated in 1978 that he had at first believed that the constitution of 1945 was essentially a standby document that would probably have to be rewritten twenty years later, but he subsequently changed his mind and emphasized that the amendment process seemed capable of providing the necessary updating of the constitution. He summed up the process by stating, "Missouri's genius for incremental political adjustment thus takes on the character of a comfortable Guardian Angel, or behind-the-scenes

Work Horse, that keeps the functions and services responding fairly effectively while suffering through reformist outcries, cleansing elections, and constitutional surgeries."[4] Still today this is a very accurate description of the Missouri political and constitutional processes. Observers have viewed Missouri as a conservative state that emphasizes individualism resulting in a philosophy of limited government and a careful, cautious approach to problems of public policy. If this is an accurate representation of the character of the state, the Missouri Constitution fits quite well into the state's overall political environment.

Notes

1. The Missouri State Constitution

1. William L. Bradshaw, "Missouri's Proposed New Constitution," *American Political Science Review* 39 (1945): 61–65. Historic material also from William Parrish, Charles Jones, and Lawrence Christiansen, *Missouri: The Heart of the Nation,* 3rd ed. (Wheeling, Ill.: Forum Press, 2005); and Ronald Brecke and Greg Plumb, "Missouri Constitutionalism: Meandering toward Progress, 1820–2004," in *The Constitutionalism of American States,* edited by George E. Connor (Columbia: University of Missouri Press, 2008).

2. Martin Faust, *Constitution Making in Missouri: The Convention of 1943–1945* (New York: National Municipal League, 1971).

3. Council of State Governments, *Book of the States* (Lexington, Ky.: Council of State Governments, 2009), 10.

4. Lawrence M. Friedman, "State Constitutions in Historical Perspective," *Annals of the American Academy of Political and Social Science* (March 1988): 33.

5. Joseph R. Grodin, *In Pursuit of Justice: Reflections of a State Supreme Court Justice* (Berkeley and Los Angeles: University of California Press, 1989), xviii.

6. G. Alan Tarr and Mary Cornelia Porter, "Introduction: State Constitutionalism and State Constitutional Law," *Publius: The Journal of Federalism* 17 (Winter 1987): 1; John Kincaid, "The New Judicial Federalism," *Journal of State Government* 61 (September–October 1988): 13–69.

7. Judith S. Kaye, "Contributions of State Constitutional Law to the Third Century of American Federalism," *Vermont Law Review* 13 (Spring 1988): 49–60; Judith S. Kaye, "The Interpretation of State Constitutional Rights," *Harvard Law Review* 95 (April 1982): 1326–1496; John Kincaid, "State Constitutions in the Federal System," *Annals of the American Academy of Political and Social Science* (March 1988): 12–22.

8. *State v. Lowry,* 295 Or. 337, 667 P. 2d 996, 1013 (1983) (Jones, J., concurring specially).

2. The Bill of Rights and Distribution of Powers

1. Conrad Paulsen, "State Constitutions, State Courts, and First Amendment Freedoms," *Vanderbilt Law Review* 4 (April 1951): 642; William Brennan, "State Constitutional Law," *National Law Journal* (September 29, 1986): special section at 5-1.

2. *Three Rivers Junior College Dist. at Poplar Bluff v. Statler,* 421 S.W. 2d 235 (Mo. banc 1967).

3. *GEM Stores, Inc. v. O'Brien,* 364 S.W. 2d 109 (Mo. banc 1964).

4. *Independent Store Company v. Higdon,* 572 S.W. 2d 424 (Mo. banc 1978).

5. *Asher v. Lombardi,* 877 S.W. 2d 630 (Mo. banc 1994).

6. *King v. Swenson,* 423 S.W. 2d 699 (Mo. banc 1968); *Adams v. Children's Mercy Hosp.,* 832 S.W. 2d 898 (Mo. banc 1992).

7. *Cooper v. Board of Probation and Parole,* 866 S.W. 2d 135 (Mo. banc 1993).

8. John Devlin, "Constructing an Alternative to 'State Action' as a Limit to State Constitutional Rights Guarantees: A Survey, Critique, and Proposal," *Rutgers Law Journal* 21, no. 4 (1990): 842n113, 851n158.

9. *Barber v. Time, Inc.,* 159 S.W. 2d 294 (Mo. S. Ct. Div. 1 1942).

10. *Cruzan v. Harmon,* 760 S.W. 2d 400 (Mo. banc 1988); *Cruzan v. Missouri Director of Public Health,* 497 U.S. 261 (1990).

11. *McDonnough v. Aylward,* 500 S.W. 2d 723 (Mo. S. Ct. Div. 1 1973).

12. *Association for Educational Development v. Hazward,* 533 S.W. 2d 587 (Mo. banc 1976).

13. *Paster v. Tussey,* 512 S.W. 2d 104 (Mo. banc 1974); *Lemon v. Kurtzman,* 91 U.S. 2105 (1971). The *Lemon* decision allows for some government aid if the statute (1) has a secular purpose, (2) its principal or primary effect is one that neither advances nor inhibits religion, and (3) there is no excessive government entanglement with religion.

14. *McVey v. Hawkins,* 258 S.W. 2d 927 (Mo. banc 1953); *Everson v. Board of Ed.,* 67 U.S. 504 (1947); *Luethkemeyer et al. v. Kaufmann,* 95 U.S. 167 (1974).

15. *Waite v. Waite,* 567 S.W. 2d 326 (Mo. banc 1978).

16. *Wheeler v. Barrera,* 95 U.S. 2284–85 (1973).

17. *In Search Warrant of Property at West 12th Street v. Marcus,* 334 S.W. 2d 119 (Mo. banc 1960); *Marcus v. Search Warrants of Property,* 81 U.S. 1708 (1961).

18. *State v. Simmer,* 772 S.W. 2d 373 (Mo. banc 1989); *Miller v. California,* 413 U.S. 15 (1973).

19. *State v. Roberts,* 779 S.W. 2d 579 (Mo. banc 1989); *BBC Fireworks v. State Highway and Transportation Commission,* 828 S.W. 2d 882–83 (Mo. banc 1992).

20. *In re. Westfall,* 808 S.W. 2d 829 (Mo. banc 1993).

21. *Caldwell Banker Residential Real Estate Serv., Inc. v. Missouri Real Estate Commission,* 712 S.W. 2d 666 (Mo. banc 1986).

22. *Rollins v. Shannon,* 292 F. Supp. 580 (1968).

23. *State v. Bradford,* 262 S.W. 2d 589 (Mo. S. Ct. Div. 1 1953).

24. *In re Elliston,* 789 S.W. 2d 469 (Mo. banc 1990).

25. *State ex rel. Stanhope v. Platt,* 533 S.W. 2d 575 (Mo. banc 1976).

26. *State ex rel. Stearns v. White,* 189 S.W. 2d 206 (Springfield Ct. of Appeals 1985).

27. *State ex rel. Cavallaro v. Groose,* 862 S.W. 2d 338 (Mo. banc 1995).

28. Note in addition, Article III, Section 40.

29. *Doe v. Roman Catholic Diocese,* 862 S.W. 2d 338 (Mo. banc 1993).

30. *Doe v. Phillips,* 194 S.W. 3d 833 (Mo. banc 2006).

31. *State ex rel. Cardinal Glennon Memorial Hospital for Children v. Gaertner,* 583 S.W. 2d 110 (Mo. banc 1979).

32. *Mahoney v. Doerhoff Surgical Services*, 807 S.W. 2d 503 (Mo. banc 1979).

33. *Findley v. City of Kansas City*, 782 S.W. 2d 393 (Mo. banc 1989).

34. *Simpson v. Rilcher*, 794 S.W. 2d 389 (Mo. banc 1988).

35. *State v. Jefferson*, 391 S.W. 2d 888 (Mo. banc 1965).

36. *State v. Moody*, 443 S.W. 2d 803 (Mo. banc 1969); John Scarlock, "Searches and Seizures in Missouri," *University of Kansas City Law Review* 29 (1961): 255; *State v. Miller*, 894 S.W. 2d 649 (Mo. banc 1995).

37. *Matter of Interim Report of Grand Jury*, 553 S.W. 2d 482 (Mo. banc 1977).

38. *State v. Cooper*, 344 S.W. 2d 72 (Mo. banc 1961).

39. *State v. Sanchez*, 752 S.W. 2d 322–23 (Mo. banc 1998).

40. *Maryland v. Craig*, 110 U.S. 3157 (1990); *State v. Hester*, 801 S.W. 2d 695 (Mo. banc 1991); *State v. Nancke*, 829 S.W. 2d 456 (Mo. banc 1992); *State v. Schaal*, 806 S.W. 2d 356 (Mo. banc 1991).

41. *State v. Dunn*, 817 S.W. 2d 244 (Mo. banc 1991).

42. *State v. Lindsey*, 578 S.W. 2d 904 (Mo. banc 1979).

43. *State v. Sumlin*, 820 S.W. 2d 487 (Mo. banc 1991).

44. *State v. McTush*, 827 S.W. 2d 186 (Mo. banc 1992).

45. Wayne R. Lafave and Jerold H. Israel, *Criminal Procedure* (St. Paul: West Publishing, 1985), 551.

46. *Hickman v. O'Connell*, 266 S.W. 2d 10 (Mo. St. Louis Ct. of Appeals 1954).

47. *Duisen v. State*, 441 S.W. 2d 693 (Mo. banc 1969); *Gregg v. Georgia*, 428 U.S. 153 (1976).

48. *State ex rel. Cox v. Wilson*, 435 S.W. 2d 658 (Mo. S. Ct. Div. 2 1968).

49. *State v. Butts*, 159 S.W. 2d 793 (Mo. banc 1942).

50. *State v. Hudley*, 815 S.W. 2d 422 (Mo. banc 1991).

51. *State v. Powell*, 798 S.W. 2d 709 (Mo. banc 1990); *State v. McMillin*, 783 S.W. 2d 82 (Mo. banc 1989).

52. *State v. Storey*, 901 S.W. 2d 892 (Mo. banc 1995).

53. *State v. Griffith*, 756 S.W. 2d 475 (Mo. banc 1988).

54. *State v. Goree*, 762 S.W. 2d 20 (Mo. banc 1988).

55. *Duren v. Missouri*, 99 U.S. 664 (1979).

56. Edward H. Hunvold Jr., "A Dialogue on the Application of Federal Standards to Missouri Criminal Law," *Missouri Law Review* 30 (Spring 1965): 350.

57. *State v. Keet*, 190 S.W. 2d 574 (Mo. S. Ct. Div. 2 1916). Then *Brooks v. Missouri*, 128 S.W. 3d 844 (Mo. banc 2004) with the broad interpretation.

58. *Alvin Brooks v. State of Missouri Attorney General Jeremiah Nixon*, 128 S.W. 2d 674 (Mo. banc 2004).

59. 571.020 RSMo. 2008.

60. *Griswold v. Connecticut*, 85 U.S. 1678 (1965).

61. *State ex rel. McClellan v. Kirkpatrick*, 504 S.W. 2d 89 (Mo. banc 1974).

62. *Board of Regents of Northwest Missouri State Teacher's College v. Palmer*, 204 S.W. 2d 293–94 (Mo. S. Ct. Div. 2 1947).

63. See Sections 523–62 RSMo. 2008; and Stanley Leasure, "Eminent Domain: Missouri's Response to *Kelo*," *Journal of the Missouri Bar* (July–August 2007). See also *Albright Properties, Inc. v. Tax Increment Financing Commission of Kansas City*, 240 S.W. 3d 777 (Mo. banc 2007); and 523.271 RSMo. 2008.

64. J. Nelson Happy, "*Damnum Absque Injuria:* When Private Property May Be

Damaged without Compensation in Missouri," *Missouri Law Review* 36 (Fall 1971): 453–70.

65. *Missouri Highway Transportation Commission v. Horne*, 776 S.W. 2d 10 (Mo. banc 1989).

66. *Heins Implement v. Highway Transportation Commission*, 589 S.W. 2d 281 (Mo. banc 1993).

67. *State ex rel. C. F. White and Family v. Roldan*, 271 S.W. 3d 569 (Mo. banc 2008).

68. *Clinics and Hospitals v. McConnell*, 236 S.W. 2d 390 (Mo. Kansas City Ct. of Appeals 1951).

69. *Roberts v. City of Maryville*, 750 S.W. 2d 70 (Mo. banc 1988).

70. *State ex rel. U.S. Steel v. Koehr*, 811 S.W. 2d 289 (Mo. banc 1991).

71. See Sections 523–62 RSMo. 2008.

72. *Missouri Highway and Transportation Commission v. Horne*.

73. *State ex rel. Missey v. City of Cabool*, 441 S.W. 2d 390 (Mo. banc 1991).

74. *Independence–National Education Association et al. v. Independence School District*, 223 S.W. 3d 131 (Mo. banc 2007).

75. *McDermott v. Nations*, 580 S.W. 2d 253 (Mo. banc 1979).

76. *State v. Dishman*, 68 S.W. 2d 797–98 (Mo. banc 1934).

77. *Otto v. Kansas City*, 276 S.W. 389 (Mo. banc 1925).

78. *Clark v. Austin*, 101 S.W. 2d 977 (Mo. banc 1937).

79. *State v. Cushman*, 451 S.W. 2d 17 (Mo. banc 1970).

80. *Rhodes v. Bell*, 130 S.W. 2d 465 (Mo. banc 1910).

81. *State ex rel. Cuson v. Bond*, 495 S.W. 2d 385 (Mo. banc 1973).

82. *State ex inf. McKitrick ex rel. Ham v. Kirby*, 163 S.W. 2d 990 (Mo. banc 1942).

83. *Edwards v. Schoemehl*, 765 S.W. 2d 608 (Mo. banc 1989).

3. The Legislature

1. *State ex inf. v. State Environmental Improvement Authority*, 518 S.W. 2d 68 (Mo. banc 1979).

2. *Reynolds v. Sim*, 84 U.S. 1362 (1964).

3. Fred W. Lindecke, "Remapping May Hold Surprises," *St. Louis Post-Dispatch*, October 8, 1989.

4. *Stiles v. Hicky*, 475 S.W. 617 (Mo. banc 1972).

5. Ibid.; *State v. Banks*, 454 S.W. 2d 498 (Mo. banc 1970).

6. *State ex rel. Garlike v. Walsh*, 483 S.W. 2d 70 (Mo. banc 1972).

7. *U.S. Term Limits, Inc. v. Thornton*, 115 U.S. 1842 (1995).

8. *State ex rel. Atkinson v. Planned Indus. Expansion Authority of St. Louis*, 517 S.W. 2d 36 (Mo. banc 1975).

9. *State ex rel. Garlike v. Walsh*.

10. *State ex rel. Bunker Resource Recycling and Reclamation, Inc. v. Mehan*, 782 S.W. 2d 381 (Mo. banc 1990).

11. *Harris v. Missouri Gaming Commission*, 869 S.W. 2d 58 (Mo. banc 1994).

12. *Hunter Avenue Property v. Union Electric Co.*, 869 S.W. 2d 146 (Mo. App. E. D. 1995).

13. Patrick Cronan, "Special Legislation: May Not Obey the State Constitution?" *Governmental Affairs Newsletter* 26, no. 2 (1991): 5–8; Patrick Cronan, "How

Do You Spell . . ." [general wording for special legislation adopted in 1991 session], *Governmental Affairs Newsletter* 26, no. 2 (1991): 8–9.

14. *School District v. St. Louis County,* 816 S.W. 2d 219 (Mo. banc 1972); *Hanson v. State of Missouri,* 226 S.W. 3d 137 (Mo. banc 2007); *Anderson et al. v. State of Missouri,* 273 S.W. 3d 370 (Mo. banc 2009).

15. Lindecke, "Remapping May Hold Surprises."

16. *Scott v. Kirkpatrick,* 513 S.W. 2d 442 (Mo. banc 1974).

17. *State ex rel. Upchurch v. Blunt,* 810 S.W. 2d 515 (Mo. banc 1991).

18. *Liberty Oil Co. v. Director of Revenue,* 813 S.W. 2d 296 (Mo. banc 1991); *State v. Knapp,* 843 S.W. 2d 345 (Mo. banc 1992).

19. *State v. Knapp.*

4. The Executive Department

1. Michael Engel, *State and Local Politics* (New York: St. Martins, 1985), 86.

2. *State ex rel. King v. Walsh,* 484 S.W. 2d 644 (Mo. banc 1972).

3. *State ex rel. Cason v. Bond,* 495 S.W. 2d 392 (Mo. banc 1973).

4. Council of State Governments, *Book of the States* (Lexington, Ky.: Council of State Governments, 2007), 30:43–46).

5. *State v. Cason,* 507 S.W. 2d 413–14 (Mo. banc 1973).

6. *State ex rel. John D. Ashcroft v. Blunt,* 813 S.W. 2d 849 (Mo. banc 1991).

7. *State ex rel. Crittenden v. Walker,* 78 Mo. 139 (1883).

8. 29.0 RSMo. 2008.

9. 28.0 RSMo. 2008.

10. 30.0 RSMo. 2008.

11. 27.0 RSMo. 2008.

12. *Gershmann Investment Corp. v. Danforth,* 517 S.W. 2d 33 (Mo. banc 1974).

13. 351.0 RSMo. 2008.

14. 106.250 RSMo. 2008.

15. 32.0 RSMo. 2008.

16. *Mo. Outdoor Adv. v. Highway and Transportation Commission,* 826 S.W. 2d 345 (Mo. banc 1992).

17. 261.0 RSMo. 2008.

18. 620.0 RSMo. 2008.

19. 660.0 RSMo. 2008.

20. 630.0 RSMo. 2008.

21. 252.0 RSMo. 2008.

22. 640.0 RSMo. 2008.

23. 650.0 RSMo. 2008.

24. 286.0 RSMo. 2008.

25. 37.0 RSMo. 2008.

26. 73.0 RSMo. 2008.

27. 161.0 RSMo. 2008.

28. 217.0 RSMo. 2008, 192.0 RSMo. 2008.

29. The conservation tax spending was challenged in court as a violation of the Hancock Amendment protocols. The court separated it out as separate from the Hancock limitations in *Conservation Federation of Missouri v. Hanson, Cole County,* 994 S.W. 2d 27 (Mo. banc 2008).

5. The Judiciary

1. Grodin, *In Pursuit of Justice*, xiv–xv (see intro., n. 5).

2. *Supreme Court of Missouri* (Jefferson City: Supreme Court of Missouri, July 1987).

3. *Carter v. Director of Revenue*, 805 S.W. 2d 154 (Mo. banc 1991); *House of Lloyd v. Director of Revenue*, 824 S.W. 2d 914 (Mo. banc 1992).

4. *Asbury v. Lombardi*, 846 S.W. 2d 200 (Mo. banc 1993).

5. *State v. Mahurin*, 799 S.W. 2d 842 (Mo. banc 1990).

6. *Zahner v. City of Percyville*, 813 S.W. 2d 858 (Mo. banc 1990).

7. *State ex rel. Union Electric Co. v. Barnes*, 893 S.W. 2d 805 (Mo. banc 1995).

8. *Reed v. Labor and Industrial Relations Commission*, 789 S.W. 2d 19 (Mo. banc 1990).

9. *Conservation Federation of Missouri v. Hanson, Cole County* (see chap. 4, n. 29). See also Virginia Young, "Court Losing the Great Dissenter," *St. Louis Post-Dispatch*, September 5, 1989.

10. *Yellow Freight System v. Mayor's Commission*, 791 S.W. 2d 382 (Mo. banc 1990).

11. 49.020 RSMo. 2008.

12. *Jarvis v. Director of Revenue*, 894 S.W. 2d 22 (Mo. banc 1991).

13. *In re Ellison*, 789 S.W. 2d 469 (Mo. banc 1990).

14. Edward H. Kohn, "State High Court Judges Assail Disciplinary Panel," *St. Louis Post-Dispatch*, July 10, 1987; Robert P. Sigman, "Ill-tempered, Rude Judges Aren't Above Rebuke," *Kansas City Star*, August 16, 1990.

15. Jerry Brekke, "There Goes the Judge: Retirement, Removal, and Discipline of Judges," *Comparative State Politics* 17, no. 1 (1996): 38–45.

16. *Republican Party of Minnesota v. White*, 536 U.S. 765 (2002).

17. *Gregory v. Ashcroft*, 111 U.S. 2395 (1991).

6. Miscellaneous Articles: Articles VI–XIII

1. *State ex rel. City of Elisville v. St. Louis County Board of Election Commissioners*, 877 S.W. 2d 620 (Mo. banc 1994).

2. 48.020 RSMo. 2008.

3. 50.333 RSMo. 2008.

4. 72 RSMo. 2008.

5. *Heater v. Burt*, 769 S.W. 2d 127 (Mo. banc 1989).

6. *Brawley v. McNary*, 811 S.W. 2d 367 (Mo. banc 1991).

7. *School District v. St. Louis County*, 816 S.W. 2d 219 (Mo. banc 1990).

8. *Millsap v. Quinn*, 785 S.W. 2d 82 (Mo. banc 1990).

9. *Matter of Impeachment of Moriarty*, 902 S.W. 2d 273 (Mo. banc 1994).

10. *State ex inf. Attorney General v. Shull*, 887 S.W. 2d 128 (Mo. banc 1994).

11. 115.139 RSMo. 2008 established registration procedures. *Weinschenck v. State*, 203 S.W. 3d 201 (Mo. banc 2006), denied the use of photo IDs.

12. *Marre v. Reed*, 775 S.W. 2d 423 (Mo. banc 1989).

13. *Committee for Educational Equality et al., Coalition to Fund Excellent Schools et al. v. State of Missouri*, 294 S.W. 3d 477 (Mo. banc 2009).

14. *Reorganized School District No. 7 v. Douthit*, 799 S.W. 2d 591 (Mo. banc 1990).

15. *Gage & Tucker v. Director of Revenue*, 769 S.W. 2d 119 (Mo. banc 1989).

16. *Schnorbus v. Director of Revenue*, 790 S.W. 2d 241 (Mo. banc 1990).

17. *Associated Ind. v. Director of Revenue*, 887 S.W. 2d 182 (Mo. banc 1993).

18. *Land Clearance for Redevelopment Authority v. Waris*, 790 S.W. 2d 454 (Mo. banc 1990).

19. *United Cerebral Palsy Association v. Ross*, 789 S.W. 2d 798 (Mo. banc 1990).

20. David Burch, "The Hancock Amendment Revisited," *Governmental Affairs Newsletter* 15, no. 7 (March 1981): 7–8; "More Reflections on the Hancock Amendment," *Governmental Affairs Newsletter* 17, no. 7 (March 1983): 4–6. See also *Franklin County ex rel. Parks v. Franklin County Commission*, 269 S.W. 3d 26 (Mo. banc 2008); and *Missouri Association of Counties et al. v. Quentin Wilson et al.*, 3 S.W. 3d 772 (Mo. banc 1999).

21. Office of the State Auditor of Missouri, *Review of Article X, Sections 16 through 24, Constitution of Missouri* (Jefferson City: Office of the State Auditor of Missouri, June 30, 1995).

22. *Buchner v. Bond*, 650 S.W. 2d 611 (Mo. banc 1983).

23. *Roberts v. McNary*, 636 S.W. 2d 332 (Mo. banc 1982).

24. 67.042 RSMo. 2008.

25. *Beatty v. Metro. St. Louis Sewer District*, 867 S.W. 2d 217 (Mo. banc 1993); *Freese v. City of Lake Ozark, Mo.*, 893 S.W. 2d 810 (Mo. banc 1995).

26. *Rolla 31 School District v. State*, 837 S.W. 2d 5–6 (Mo. banc 1992).

27. *State ex rel. Upchurch v. Blunt* (see chap. 3, n. 17).

28. *Missourians to Protect Initiative Process v. Blunt*, 799 S.W. 2d 824 (Mo. banc 1990).

Conclusion: An Evolving Document

1. Parrish, Jones, and Christiansen, *Missouri* (see intro., n. 1).

2. Martin L. Faust, "Constitutional Convention in Missouri?" *Business and Government Review* 3, no. 2 (1962): 17–21.

3. William F. Swindler, "Missouri Constitutions: History, Theory, and Practice," *Missouri Law Review* 23 (April 1958): 157–79.

4. Robert F. Karsch, *The Government of Missouri* (Columbia: Lucas Brothers, 1978).

Index

About the Authors

Richard Fulton is Professor of Political Science at Northwest Missouri State University and the author or editor of several books, including *The WTO Primer: Tracing Trade's Invisible Hand through Case Studies*. Jerry Brekke is Professor Emeritus of Political Science at Northwest Missouri State University and the author of *Understanding the Missouri Constitution*.